nifty thrifty

Bible Crafts

Animals of the Old Testament

Special Thanks

This book is dedicated to my loving husband, Nicholas, who unselfishly gave of his time and wisdom in helping to make my dreams come true. I would also like to thank my family, co-workers and closest friends, Trisha, Marylou, Sony and all my prayer warriors, who not only encouraged me to never give up but, to stay focused on God's will: *Keeping Christ Alive in our Kids!* Lastly, I want to thank all the Sunday school classes at First Baptist Church, who helped *Nifty Thrifty Bible Crafts*, become a huge success!

Donna Gentile

nifty thrifty

Bible Crafts

Animals of the Old Testament

Donna Gentile

A Way of Life Publishing LLC

www.awayoflifepublishing.com

Nifty Thrifty Bible Crafts: Animals Of The Old Testament
Copyright © 2013 by A Way of Life Publishing LLC, first printing

ISBN 10: 0-9888356-0-6
ISBN 13: 978-0-9888356-0-3

RELIGION/Christian Ministry/Children

A Way of Life Publishing LLC
P.O. Box 1236
Slidell, LA 70459-1236

Visit our Web site: www.awayoflifepublishing.com

Publishing Manager: Nicholas Gentile
Editor: Victoria Denise Bonilla
Copy Editor: Trisha Crombie
Illustrator: Rick Incrocci
Cover Design: Diane Bay

Library of Congress Control Number: 2013941984

Printed in the United States of America

TABLE OF CONTENTS

CHARACTER BUILDERS
(Memory Verses)

Attentive (Horse)

Blessed is the man who listens to me, watching daily at my doors, waiting at my doorway

(Proverbs 8:34) 81

Bold (Snake)

The Lord is with me; he is my helper. I will look in triumph on my enemies

(Psalm 118:7) 44

Faithful (Cow)

We live by faith, not by sight

(2 Corinthians 5:7) 39

Grateful (Monkey)

I praise you because I am fearfully and wonderfully made ...

(Psalm 139:14) 11

Helpful (Whale)

Brothers, if someone is caught in a sin, you who are spiritual should restore him gently ...

(Galatians 6:1) 92

Hopeful (Quail)

Why are you downcast, O my soul? Why so disturbed within me? Put your hope in God ...

(Psalm 42:5) 61

Hospitable (Raven)

Share with God's people who are in need. Practice hospitality

(Romans 12:13) 76

Joyful (Frog)

Worship the Lord with gladness; come before him with joyful songs

(Psalm 100:2) 49

Kindness (Camel)

Love is patient, love is kind ...

(1 Corinthians 13:4) 33

Loyal (Donkey)

A friend loves at all times ...

(Proverbs 17:17) 66

Obedient (Giraffe)

Follow my decrees and be careful to obey my laws, and you will live safely in the land

(Leviticus 25:18) 21

Patient (Dove)

Be joyful in hope, patient in affliction, faithful in prayer

(Romans 12:12) 28

Resourceful (Bee)

And my God will meet all your needs according to his glorious riches in Christ Jesus

(Philippians 4:19) 71

Respectful (Lamb)

If you do what is right, will you not be accepted? But if you do not do what is right, sin is crouching at your door; it desires to have you, but you must master it

(Genesis 4:7) 16

Responsible (Locust)

Whatever you do, work at it with all your heart, as working for the Lord, not for men

(Colossians 3:23) 56

Unselfish (Lion)

Each of you should look not only to your own interests, but also to the interests of others

(Philippians 2:4) 86

INTRODUCTION

Parents! Are you looking for ways to jumpstart your children's creativity? Teachers! Do your students love creating crafts? Are you searching for crafts that are fun, yet easy on your budget?

Whether for Sunday school, Vacation Bible school or home, *Nifty Thrifty Bible Crafts: Animals of the Old Testament* provides 32 time-saving *reproducible craft patterns*, *16 Bible stories* and *Character Builder Memory Verses* that teach God's word in a fun and creative way.

HOW TO USE THIS BOOK

Begin challenging children's inquisitiveness by asking them to listen for clues within the Bible story (e.g. colors, shapes or sounds) as to which Old Testament animal is narrating the story. Instruct them to hold back the animal's identity until a question similar to: *Can you guess what animal I am yet?* is asked. After the animal's identity is revealed, show them the Bible story illustration. Utilize the *Character Builder Memory Verses* and *Can You Guess the Answer* questions to build new Godly character (*e.g.,* kindness, respectful or helpful).

Next, follow-up with one of the hands-on, interactive, reproducible crafts (ages 5-10) (adapt for younger, older or special needs children). Each Craft Instruction Page displays:

SUPPLIES: common household, recyclable or school craft supplies

PREPS: quick pre-craft suggestions

E-Z STEPS: easy step-by-step craft instructions

TEACHABLES: challenges children to practice Godly character qualities.

God bless you on your efforts to expose children to a unique way of learning God's word. Thanks for *Keeping Christ Alive in our Kids!*

Grateful

* * * * * * * * *

Memory Verse

*I praise you because I am fearfully and
wonderfully made ... (Psalm 139:14)*

It's Time to Celebrate!

Based on Genesis 1:20-30

* * * * * * * * * * * * * *

*Roarrr! [pause] Mooooo! [pause] Bzzzzzz!
[pause]* "What are those sounds I hear?"
As I slowly open my eyes, whoa! What an
awesome sight! There are wild animals,
livestock, and crawling creatures everywhere. I hear it's the fifth day of the creation of the
world and God has just finished creating the animals to look, act, and sound unique.

Do you know what that means? Today's my birthday. It's time to celebrate. *Ooh ooh ah ah!*
Where's that funny sound coming from? Hey, that's me! I sure sound funny and look funny
too. I am hairy all over, with short legs, long arms, a flat face, and big ears. God created me
special to make others laugh. Whether with funny faces or jumping up and down with an *ooh
ooh* here and an *ah ah* there, I love making others laugh. *Can you guess what animal I am
yet? [pause]*

"Let's celebrate our creation," I told the others. "How do I get down from here?" I wonder.
Let's see. Maybe if I curl this long tail of mine around this branch while swinging over to
grab hold of this branch...oops! I missed and, like an acrobat, ooooh! My body began to twirl
uncontrollably. I tried to grab hold again, this time I came to an abrupt stop. Whew! That
was close. I think I finally got the hang of this now. As I swing from tree to tree, dangling in
mid-air, I'm startled by the magnificent voice of God: "I will make man in My own image and
let him rule over the fish of the sea and the birds of the air and over every creature on the
ground."

In utter awe, I watch as God creates Adam, the man, and Eve, the woman, in His own image.
He blesses them and says: "Be fruitful, increase in number, and enjoy food from the seed-
bearing plants and fruit-bearing trees."

Ooh, ooh, aah, aah! Watching God create has sure made me hungry! Ahhh is that my favorite
yellow fruity snack I see? A banana? Yum! While I sit and enjoy, Adam names all of the wild
animals, livestock, and crawling creatures in God's newly created world.

Night is almost here. Curiously, I watch the whale come up for air and the sea otters perform
their favorite backstroke, and I thank God for how fearfully and wonderfully He made us,
especially a funny monkey like me!

Can You Guess The Answer?

1. On what day of creation did God create the animals?
2. What makes you special from others that you can be grateful to God for?

Yeah! Created in God's Image

Supplies

brown sticky back craft foam
yellow sticky back craft foam
pencil
scissors
resealable plastic bag
craft glue
black permanent marker

Preps

Reproduce Monkey Parts on page 13.
Lay Monkey Parts page over the
appropriate colored craft foam and using
the tip of the pencil, trace the outline of
each Monkey Part to the appropriate
colored craft foam. Cut out Psalm 139:14
verse and all craft foam Monkey Parts and place in a resealable plastic bag, one
set per child. Create a sample craft for children to view.

E-Z Steps

1. Ask children to remove the Psalm 139:14 verse and all craft foam Monkey
   Parts from their resealable plastic bags.

2. Hold up sample craft. Show them where to glue the yellow face on to the
   brown monkey body, the yellow mouth to the yellow face, the brown nose to
   the top of the yellow mouth and lastly, the yellow ears on the right and left
   side of the yellow face. Point to the monkey's feet, eyes, mouth, arm separator
   and black tips on the banana. Using the black permanent marker, ask the
   children to draw these features on their monkey.

3. Show the children where to glue the banana and the Psalm 139:14 verse.

4. Have children look up and discuss Psalm 139:14, allowing time for craft to
   dry.

Teachables

Encourage children to hang or attach their monkey to a special place at home, as
remembrance too always praise Him for being fearfully and wonderfully made!

I praise you because
I am fearfully and
wonderfully made
(Psalm 139:14)

ears

banana

yellow
craft
foam

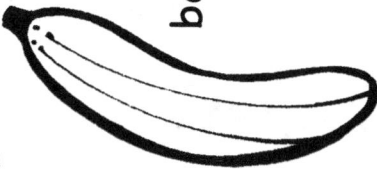

Monkey Parts

mouth

nose

arm separator

face
here

face

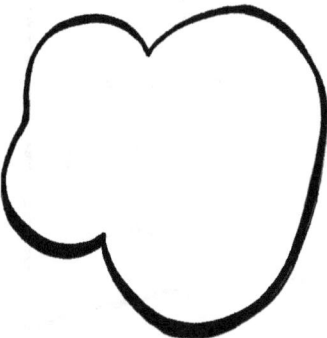

Psalm 139:14
verse goes here

body

I praise you because
I am fearfully and
wonderfully made
(Psalm 139:14)

brown
craft
foam

Thank You Card

Supplies

colored cardstock
scissors
pencil or markers
fabric paints

Preps

Reproduce the Thank You Card on page 15 on to colored cardstock for each child. Create a sample craft for children to view.

E-Z Steps

1. Ask children to cut out and fold their Thank You Card on the dashed line.

2. Hold up sample craft. Suggest they open their card. On the right hand side, ask them to print the words, "God: Thank you God for making me special" followed by their names.

3. On the left hand side, tell them to think of and print the words describing their special uniqueness (*e.g.*, blond hair, blue eyes, tall, pretty smile).

4. Instruct children to close their card. Allow creativity in decorating the front of their cards using fabric paints. Allow plenty of time for craft to dry.

Teachables

Encourage children to show their gratefulness by saying a prayer to God, for their special uniqueness. Have children memorize and share Genesis 1:27 with others. Urge them to show their Thank You Cards to their parents.

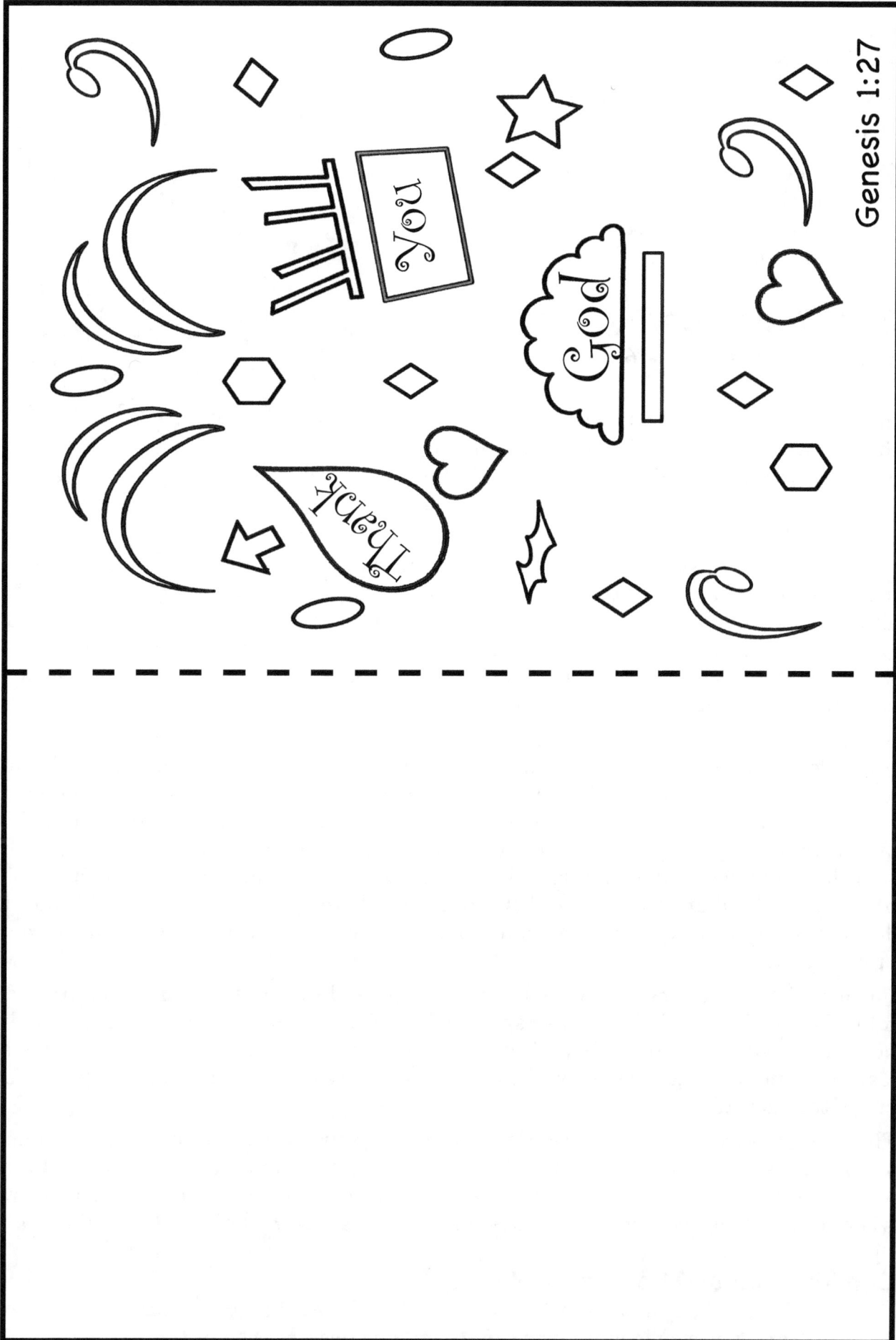

You

God

Thank

15 **Thank You Card**

Respectful

* * * * * * * * * * * * *

Memory Verse

If you do what is right, will you not be accepted? But if you do not do what is right, sin is crouching at your door; it desires to have you, but you must master it (Genesis 4:7)

Give Your Best!
Based on Genesis 4:1-16
* * * * * * * * * * * * *

In early morning, a chilly breeze blew through the tall green grass. While mamma enjoyed blades of grass, I snuggled close to her side and sipped milk from her udder. In the distance, we heard the familiar *BAAAAAA!* That's the flock's call for all male rams, female ewes, and their young, to gather round for storytelling time.

"Shhhhh!" said the storyteller, an older ram from the flock, as he lifted his hoof to us young-ins to be quiet. *Can you guess what animal we are yet? [pause]* "Let's begin," he said. "Adam and Eve, the first man and woman, were blessed with two sons, Cain and Abel. The brothers grew into men. Cain learned to grow vegetables. Abel learned to shepherd the sheep. They were taught to respect the Lord. However, tomorrow only one brother, by his offering, will win favor from the Lord. See if you can guess which one."

As curious baby sheep will be, we rose early and watched Cain offer some fruit to the Lord. Abel offered his best sheep. By the way the Lord's face lit up, we instantly knew the answer and couldn't wait for storytelling time. Finally, when it arrived, we anxiously shouted: "Abel won!" The storyteller said, "Good Job!" and asked, "Why Abel?" In an excitable high pitch lamb's voice, I answered: "Abel showed the Lord more respect by giving his best!" "Great!" said the storyteller. Later that day while we grazed, Cain's jealousy turned to anger for his brother. The Lord knew Cain was about to sin. The Lord appeared and warned Cain: "If you do what is right, will you not be accepted? But if you do not do what is right, sin is crouching at your door."

The next day, Cain's anger only grew worse. He ignored the Lord's warning and tricked Abel into following him behind some rocks in the field. The flock sensed danger. They lifted their heads and kept watch from harm. From behind the rocks, we heard loud screams and soon learned Cain killed Abel. Quickly, the flock bunched together and was led away to safety by one of the older rams.

The Lord appeared and questioned Cain: "Where is your brother?" Cain would not admit his sin. As a result, the Lord punished Cain by banning him from His presence. As Cain was leaving, he saw how I looked up to mamma with love and respect. This helped him understand where he had failed with the Lord. Lesson learned: *Respect the Lord and Give Your Best!*

Can You Guess The Answer?
1. Why did God show more favor over Abel's offering than Cain's offering?
2. Name one way in which you can "Give Your Best" to the Lord.

16

Give God Your Best Photo Frame

Supplies

camera
scissors
white cardstock
tape
sticky-back craft foam
crayons
glitter glue pens

Preps

ADVANCE NOTICE: With your camera, take each child's picture. Print and cutout each child's face proportionately to fit behind the lamb's face opening on the Front Frame, see p. 18.

Reproduce Front and Back Frames on page 18 on to white cardstock. Cut out the Frames and the lamb's face opening on the Front Frames, one Front Frame per child. Tape the reproduced Back Frame over a sheet of craft foam. Cut out the Back Frame outline and Arm where indicated to create a foam Back Frame, one Back Frame per child. Create a sample craft for children to view.

E-Z Steps

1. Ask the children to color the lamb's body on the Front Frame, leaving the white space empty around the lamb for now.
2. Tell them to center their picture behind the lamb's face opening on the Front Frame and secure with tape.
3. Instruct them to reveal the sticky side of the craft foam Back Frame. Help them join the back of the Front Frame to the sticky side of the Back Frame, pressing firmly.
4. Hold up sample craft. Encourage their creativeness. Using glitter glue pens, ask them to create designs on the white space around the lamb on the Front Frame. Allow time for craft to dry.
5. Show the children how to bend back the Frame Arm so their Give God Your Best Photo Frame can stand. Ask children to memorize Genesis 4:7.

Teachables

Give God Your Best! Learn from Abel's example. Abel chose to respect God and bring God his best sheep. Cain, on the other hand, did not give God much respect. He brought God some fruit, but not his best. God wants our best! He brings favor to those who give their best.

Front Frame

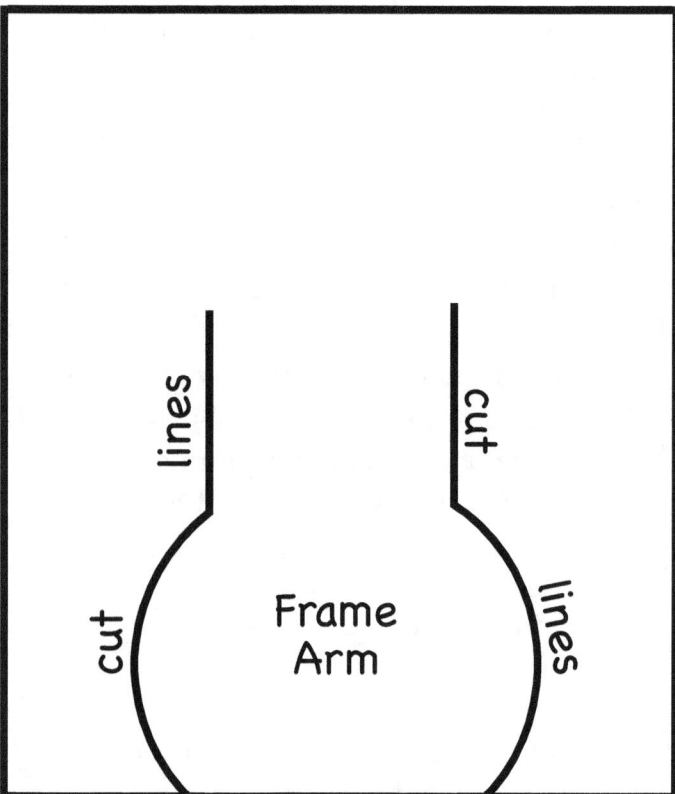

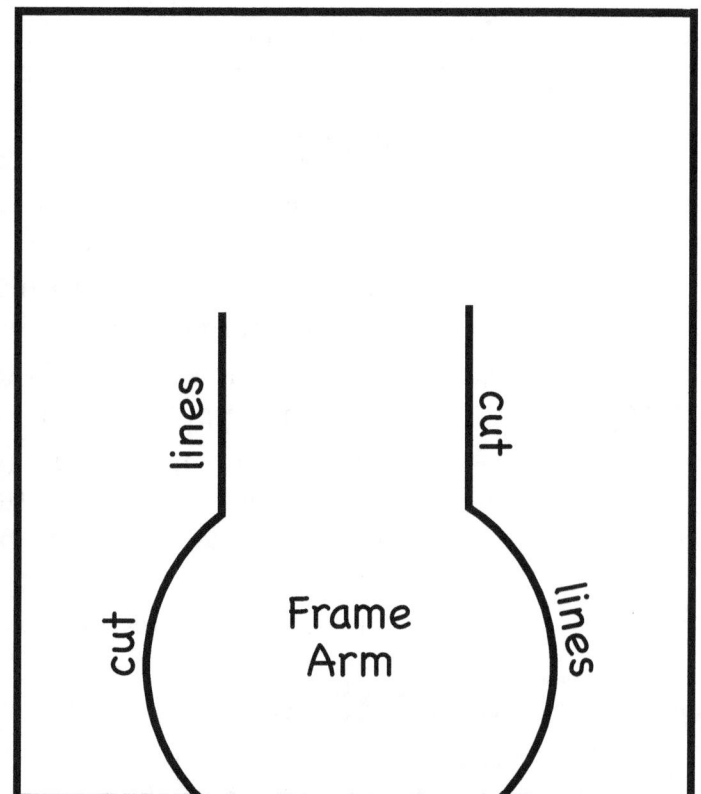

Back Frame

Create-A-Craft Party

Supplies

light colored cardstock
Give Your Best! Bible story
cupcake sprinkles
paper plates, candle
scissors, colored clay
foil cupcake holder

Preps

Reproduce the Party Invites on page 20 on to light colored cardstock, one page or four invites per child (do not cut apart). Reproduce the *Give Your Best!* Bible story on page 16 (one per child to take home) and this Craft Instruction page (one per child to take home). Pour cupcake sprinkles on to several paper plates. Create a sample craft for children to view.

E-Z Steps

1. Tell the children that they will be preparing for their own at-home Create-A-Craft Party by (1) filling out Party Invites to invite their friends and (2) by creating a sample Cupcake Candle for their guests to view. Remind children to ask for adult permission to have the party so preparations can be made in advance.

2. Hand out one page or four Party Invites per child. Suggest they print a friend's name on each blank line after the word To, their name on the From lines, and the Date and Time lines leave blank until permission is granted. Once you fill-in the Date and Time, cut out Party Invites to give to your friends.

3. Hold up sample craft. Begin creating your own sample Cupcake Candle. Form the clay into a ball. Roll one side of the clay ball into the cupcake sprinkles. Lay the clay ball inside the foil cupcake holder then insert a candle.

4. Reminders for Craft Party: Before your at-home party, gather craft supplies and prepare preps listed on the Craft Instruction page for each guest. At party time, ask an adult to read the Bible story and challenging questions under the section, Can You Guess the Answer? Hold up your sample craft while an adult reads the craft instructions. Ask your guests to create one of their own to take home. Serve light snacks and drinks and play fun Christian games.

Teachables

Have children memorize Romans 12:10, "... Honor one another above yourselves." Talk about how friends should show each other respect. Have fun at your at-home Create-A-Craft Party. Celebrate friendship!

19

Create-A-Craft
Party
Snacks   Play Games

To: _____
From: _____
Date: _____
Time: _____

Come Have Fun!

Romans
12:10

Create-A-Craft
Party
Snacks   Play Games

To: _____
From: _____
Date: _____
Time: _____

Come Have Fun!

Romans
12:10

Create-A-Craft
Party
Snacks   Play Games

To: _____
From: _____
Date: _____
Time: _____

Come Have Fun!

Romans
12:10

Create-A-Craft
Party
Snacks   Play Games

To: _____
From: _____
Date: _____
Time: _____

Come Have Fun!

Romans
12:10

Party Invites

Obedient

* * * * * * * * * * *

Memory Verse

Follow my decrees and be careful to obey my laws, and you will live safely in the land (Leviticus 25:18)

Glad We Listened to Noah

Based on Genesis 6:9-22; 7:1-24
* * * * * * * * * * * * * * * * * *

Oooh! Oooh! I can't reach those leaves at the top of the tree. "Stand on your tiptoes," my mate said. "Stretch those lanky legs and long neck. You can do it," she said. I got it! *Crunch! Crunch!* The more leaves we eat, the longer we can go without drinking water. How cool is that?

Whack! Whack! "What's that noise?" my mate asked. Noah and his sons are putting final touches on a boat called an ark. "There's no water in sight! Why are they building an ark?" she asked. Well, God appeared to Noah and warned him that He would allow rain on the earth for 40 days and 40 nights. "The people have become wicked," God said, "and a flood will wipe away everything on earth. Noah! Since you have been obedient to my laws, you and your family will be spared. Prepare ahead by building an ark of cypress wood with a roof, side door, a lower, middle and an upper deck to house two of every kind of animal, male and female." Noah obeyed God.

"It's almost time to board," Noah told his wife. Ask our daughters-in-law to help you gather food to store on the ark. Noah asked his sons to lower the huge ark door. Noah's neighbors laughed at his request and said, "Where's the water, Noah?" Noah paid no attention; he continued to obey God. Noah waved our favorite snack and we followed him into the ark. He asked for our help boarding the other animals. We didn't understand, but we obeyed. We called everything big, small, colorful, noisy or crawling thing, male and female. Noah's family boarded last and the ark door closed.

I got the job of lookout since I am the tallest and can see the farthest. I am known for my many brown spots all over my body. *Can you guess what animal I am yet? [pause]* I popped open the ark window and stuck my long giraffe neck out to look around. Noah's neighbors were still laughing as the clouds above turned very dark. *KABOOM!* A lightning strike flashed across the sky as heavy raindrops began to fall. I quickly closed the window and came inside. Noah's family cared for us as we ate, slept and played. Rain fell for 40 days and 40 nights. *Whoa!* I almost lost my balance when the ark wobbled back and forth and began to float. I no longer heard laughter outside as I opened the ark window. For as far as I could see, there were no more people, animals or trees. There was just water. Looks like we are part of a new world. *Glad we listened to Noah!*

Can You Guess The Answer?

1. Why did Noah build an ark when there was no water in sight?
2. Name one way you can be more obedient to God. Parents.

Come to
Sunday School Card

Supplies

white cardstock, two per child
scissors
crayons or markers
pencil
tape
glue
1½" brown yarn piece

Preps

Reproduce the Front of the Card
on page 23 on to one side of the
white cardstock and the Inside of the Card on page 24 on to the other side of the
white cardstock, one per child. Reproduce the Giraffe and Tab on page 25 on to
white cardstock. Fold the card in half. Open the card to be sure text has been
placed correctly during printing. Cut out the ark window on each card. Create a
sample craft for children to view.

E-Z Steps

1. Suggest children create an invitation to invite a friend to Sunday school.
2. Hold up sample craft. Instruct them to color the front of their card, as well as
   the Giraffe. Ask them to cut out the Giraffe and the Tab.
3. Tell them to open their card to print their Friend's Name and their Name,
   where indicated.
4. Ask them to slip the Giraffe neck down through the ark window on the front
   of the card. Place the Tab over the dangling neck where indicated on the
   inside of the card, then tape down the Tab sides to secure.
5. Instruct children to pull the Giraffe's neck down, apply glue where indicated,
   then cover the glue with the yarn pieces. Have them memorize Joshua 24:15,
   "... But as for me and my household, we will serve the Lord." Allow time for
   craft to dry.

Teachables

Noah, his family and the animals obeyed God. God blessed them. Obey God too
and stick your neck out for Jesus. Hand this Sunday school invitation to your
friend. After they hear the Good News, they may follow your lead and stick their
neck out too.

cut out

Joshua 24:15

COME
TO

SUNDAY
SCHOOL

"... But as for me and my household, we will serve the Lord."

Joshua 24:15

_____

[Your Name]

Come join me at Sunday school. We can learn about God, Jesus and the Bible together. We make fun crafts and take time to pray for our family and friends.

_____

[Friend's Name]

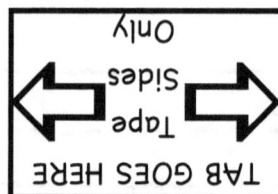

TAB GOES HERE
Tape Sides Only

Giraffe

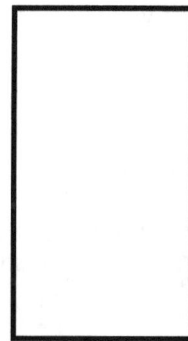

Glue yarn here

Tab

Giraffe and Tab

Obey God's Laws Wall Hanging

Supplies

white cardstock
hole punch
light colored crayons
    or markers
scissors
chenille stem
glitter glue pens
stickers

Preps

Reproduce Wall Hanging on page 27 on to white cardstock for each child. Punch holes at the top of the Wall Hanging where indicated.

Create a sample craft for children to view.

Ten Commandments

Put God First
Worship God Only
Respect God's Name
Honor the Lord's Day
Honor Parents
GOD'S LAWS
Do Not Kill
Do Not Steal
BIBLE
Do Not Lie
Keep Wedding Promises
Exodus 20:2-17 or Deuteronomy 5:6-21
Happy with What You Have
OBEY

E-Z Steps

1. Encourage the children to take turns saying one of the Ten Commandments as they color each Commandment a different color.

2. Hold up sample craft. Tell them to cut around the border of their Wall Hanging.

3. Ask them to insert each chenille stem end into a separate hole. Secure to hang.

4. Suggest the children choose the Commandments they need to improve upon.

5. Let children decorate their Wall Hanging using glitter glue pens and stickers.

Teachables

Noah was truly blessed because he chose to be obedient. Suggest children share the Ten Commandments in Exodus 20:2-17 or Deuteronomy 5:6-21 with their family. Encourage them to hang their Ten Commandments at home and to practice daily the ones they need to improve upon.

Ten Commandments

Put God First	Worship God Only

OBEY

Respect God's Name	Honor the Lord's Day

GOD'S LAWS

Honor Parents	Do Not Kill

BIBLE

Do Not Steal	Do Not Lie

Exodus 20:2–17
or
Deuteronomy 5:6–21

Keep Wedding Promises	Happy with What You Have

Patient

* * * * * * * *

Memory Verse

Be joyful in hope, patient in affliction, faithful in prayer
(Romans 12:12)

Water, Water Are You Gone?

Based on Genesis 8:1-12
* * * * * * * * * * * * *

For 40 days and 40 nights, rain tapped steadily on the roof of the ark. Noah, his wife, his three sons and their wives, and one pair of every animal, bird and crawling thing was cozy and safe inside. But outside the rain began to fall harder. The water rose higher and higher flooding the earth and those corrupted, or unwilling to obey God's laws.

With one gust of wind, the rain suddenly halted. As the water slowly lowered, cheers of "God be the glory" could be heard from inside the ark. *WHAM!* A sudden jerk was felt as the ark rested between two mountains. The passengers rose in joyful anticipation of exiting the ark. Noah quickly squashed this idea and said, "We must be sure there is dry land." Noah opened the ark window and shooed one of the larger birds, or ravens, inside the ark to fly the sky outside in search of dry land. The raven hovered above and refused to return. With no way to be sure it was safe; the passengers began to get fidgety. Noah looked to heaven in search of answers. What do you think happened?

God called upon me to fly down from one of the rafters in the ark and gracefully land on Noah's finger. Well-known as a symbol of peace, God chose me to be Noah's guide. Noah studied my gentle and patient ways. He lifted me softly to the ark window, and watched my white wings take off as I patiently glided in search of dry land. *Can you guess what animal I am yet? [pause]* Unlike the raven, I returned. Noah thought, "This must be a sign from God to be more patient." He obeyed.

Seven days later Noah again sent me in search of dry land. I returned with an olive branch in my beak, a symbol of hope that dry land was near. The passengers became anxious to exit. Noah said, "No! We must be patient, like the dove. *We must wait on God's timing and we will be blessed.*"

Seven more days passed. Noah called upon my faithful mate and me and raised us to the ark window, knowing this could be the last time he would see us. We lovingly coooed and said our beautiful goodbyes before departing. We found dry land and did not return. This was God's sign for Noah to release the passengers to live a new life on His new earth.

Can You Guess The Answer?

1. What animal did Noah study to teach him patience?
2. When you are anxious, what Bible verse do you think of to help you be more patient?

A Graceful Landing

Supplies

white cardstock
scissors
pencil
colored markers
tape
24" string

Preps

Reproduce the Dove on
page 30 on to white
cardstock for each child. Reproduce
the following verses below for children
to view OR print them on a white board:

> Be completely
> humble and
> gentle; be
> patient,
> bearing with
> one another
> in love
> Ephesians 4:2

Proverbs 19:11	*A man's wisdom gives him patience; it is to his glory to overlook an offense*
Romans 8:25	*But if we hope for what we do not yet have, we wait for it patiently*
Ephesians 4:2	*Be completely humble and gentle; be patient, bearing with one another in love*

Create a sample craft for children to view.

E-Z Steps

1. Ask the children to cut out the Dove shape.

2. Hold up sample craft. Tell them to choose one of the Bible verses regarding patience and print that Bible verse on the body of their Dove.

3. Suggest they color their Dove or leave it white like the Dove in the Bible story, Genesis 8:1-12.

4. Instruct children to tape the string to the back of the Dove's head to re-enact the graceful landing of the Dove from the Bible story.

Teachables

Encourage children to memorize the patience verse on their Dove. Have them remember the acronym: STP or Stop, Think and Be Patient. Remind them to think of the acronym STP before responding or acting upon a circumstance. Give them examples to practice STP.

Dove

Olive Branch Game

Supplies

white cardstock
scissors
pencil
colored markers

Preps

Reproduce Olive Branch Cards on page 32 on to white cardstock. Cut out the Olive Branch Cards and give two cards per child. Create a sample craft for the child to view.

E-Z Steps

1. Ask children to fill-in the blank on their Olive Branch Cards (both cards should reflect the same answer): Be patient with _____ (*e.g.*, friends, family members, classmates, neighbors).

2. Tell the children to color in the olive branch leaves on their cards.

3. Gather up all of the Olive Branch Cards (be sure no two children's answers are the same), shuffle the cards and place them face down on a table in a concentration-like game fashion.

4. Encourage children to take turns, turning over two cards, looking for like matches. If there is no match, have the child flip the cards back over than proceed to the next child until the child with the most matches WINS.

Teachables

Do you think the ark was cramped inside? Do you think they needed to exercise patience? Our homes may appear cramped and stressful at times. I wonder if they thought of Romans 12:12, "Be joyful in hope, patient in affliction, faithful in prayer." Do you have any ideas on exercising patience at home to keep peace? Home project: Every time you find yourself being impatient instead of patient, place five cents in a tithe bank to give back to the church after Sunday school class. Before long, patience will become a habit.

Be Patient
with

Romans 12:12 _____

Be Patient
with

Romans 12:12 _____

Be Patient
with

Romans 12:12 _____

Be Patient
with

Romans 12:12 _____

Be Patient
with

Romans 12:12 _____

Be Patient
with

Romans 12:12 _____

Be Patient
with

Romans 12:12 _____

Be Patient
with

Romans 12:12 _____

Olive Branch Cards

Kindness

* * * * * * * * * *

Memory Verse

Love is patient, love is kind ...
(1 Corinthians 13:4)

Be on My Best Behavior!

Based on Genesis 24
* * * * * * * * * * *

Let's have some fun! See those dates high up on this palm tree? Let's see who can stretch their neck out the farthest and eat the most! Just then, we heard voices coming from the barn. Curiously, we galloped over and heard Abraham telling his servant to travel to the town of Nabor. "Choose a wife for my son Isaac, one from my relatives and bring her back here," he said. Our long necks hugged with excitement as I said, *"Yeah! A road trip."*

The next day, the servant obeyed Abraham and prepared for the journey. He packed gifts for the relatives on ten of Abraham's best animals. He placed a riding blanket on my back as leader. "I better be on my best behavior," I thought. I better not spit or kick, as usual, when I get mad. For today, God has chosen me specially to help the servant find a wife for Isaac. "Perfect time to be kind," I thought. I began by kneeling down to make it easy for the servant to mount and ride.

Our journey to Nabor began. I led the caravan of animals in a single file fashion, first up, and then down the desert hills. Our fore and hind legs moving together, first one side, than the other. Our wide-toed hooves and big footpads helped prevent us from sinking in the sand. Our double-row eyelashes helped protect our eyes from the swirling sand. Our bodies nourished with food and water by the fat inside the humps on our back. *Can you guess what animal we are yet? [pause]*

Finally, we arrived in Nabor. Upon evening, the women were coming to draw water from the well. The servant asked me to kneel close to the well while he prayed for success: "O Lord, may it be that when I say to a girl, 'Please let down your jar that I may have a drink,' and she says, 'Drink, and I'll water your camels too' -- let her be the one you have chosen for our servant Isaac."

As the servant finished his prayer, a woman named Rebekah approached the well. The servant asked her, "Please give me a little water from your jar." She gave him a drink, turned to me and lovingly ran her fingers through my bushy eyebrows. Sensing she was the one, I fluttered my long eyelashes at her. She was in awe by my kindness and in return, kindly said, "I'll draw water for your camels too." The servant's prayer was answered. He shared why he was there. Rebekah agreed to come back to marry Isaac. To seal their agreement, the servant gave her a gold ring and bracelets. He also gave gifts to her relatives before departing. Isaac married Rebekah. "Job well done," I told the others. Now, let's go eat some sweet dates.

Can You Guess The Answer?

1. What acts of kindness did the camel show in our story?
2. What acts of kindness have you shown to others?

Mini-Care Notes

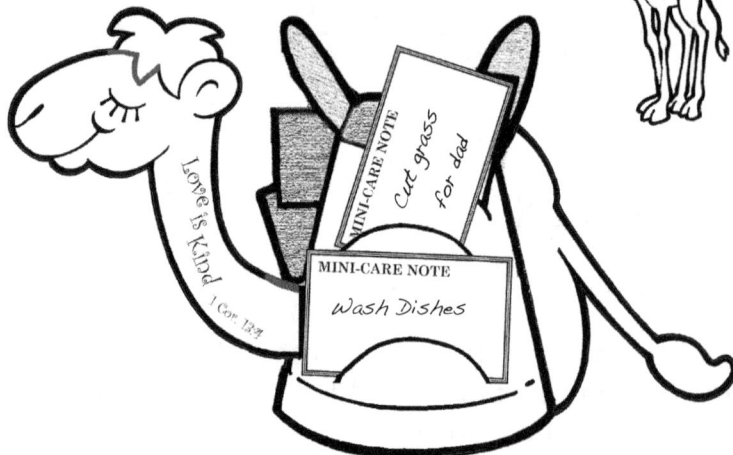

Supplies

brown construction paper
yellow cardstock
8 oz. foam cup
craft knife, scissors
clear tape, pencil

Preps

Reproduce Camel Parts on page 35 on to brown construction paper and the Mini-Care Notes on page 36 on to yellow cardstock for each child. Flip the foam cup upside down. **[SAFELY: Prepare one cup per child by following these instructions: make two slits into each cup using the craft knife: (1) vertical 1" slit above the cup's rim and (2) vertical 1" slit on the opposite side, middle of the cup. Make four 2" curved slits around the body of the cup, two on each side. See Diagram A, p. 35.]** Cut out the Mini-Care Notes, four per child. Create a sample craft for children to view.

E-Z Steps

1. Hold up sample craft. Ask children to cut out the Camel Parts (Head, Tail and Humps). With their cup upside down, instruct them to insert the Tab on the camel's Head into the 1" slit above the cup's rim and the Tab on the camel's Tail into the 1" slit on the opposite side, middle of the cup.

2. Ask them to fold on the lines where indicated on the camel's Humps in an upward direction. Tape the Humps to the flat portion of their cup.

3. Encourage them to think of four family members or friends whom they can show kindness. Tell them to print each name on to a Mini-Care Note along with one way they will show that person kindness (*e.g.,* help mom wash dishes; help Johnny with math).

4. Show the children how to press open a slit from the inside of the cup, to insert a Mini-Care Note and let go of the slit so the note stays in place. Do the same for the remaining three notes.

5. Ask the children to memorize 1 Corinthians 13:4, "Love is patient, love is kind ..."

Teachables

In our Bible story, the camel tried to be on his best behavior, a behavior unusual for a camel. Camels love to spit or kick when threatened. Our camel displayed God-like kindness to help accomplish God's purpose. Follow the camel's example. Here's a challenge. See how many times you can show kindness to someone in one day? How about a week?

Head

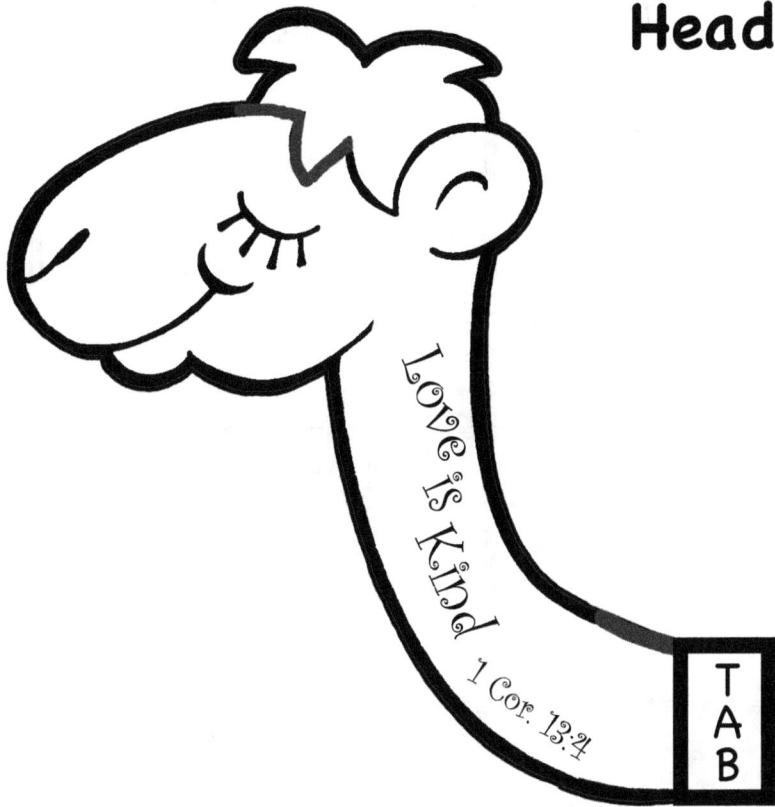

Love Is Kind 1 Cor. 13:4

TAB

Safely cut slits

Diagram A

Tail

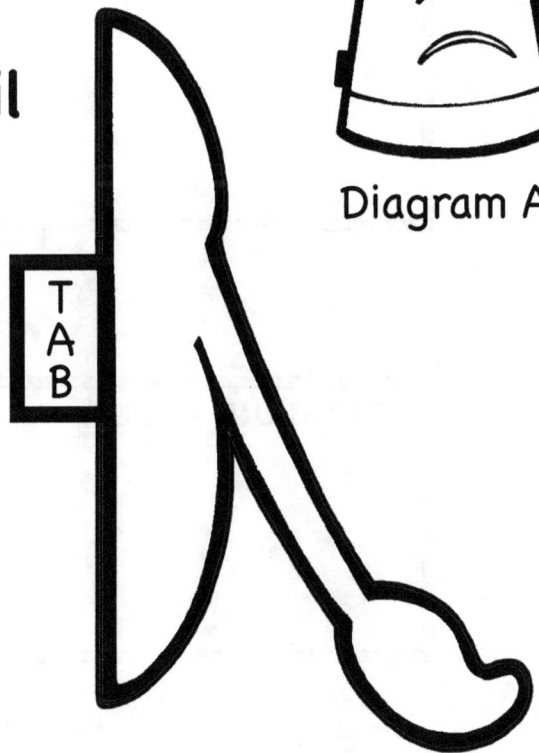

TAB

Fold Here

Fold Here

Humps

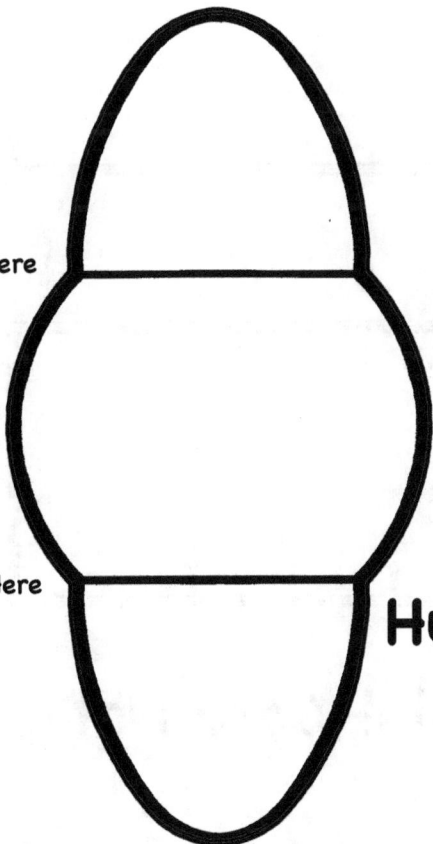

Camel Parts

MINI-CARE NOTE

MINI-CARE NOTE

MINI-CARE NOTE

MINI-CARE NOTE

MINI-CARE NOTE

MINI-CARE NOTE

MINI-CARE NOTE

MINI-CARE NOTE

Mini-Care Notes

Do for Others Notepad

Supplies

white cardstock
hole punch
red construction paper
resealable plastic bag
crayons
scissors
glue
mini-sticky notepad
pencil

Mia

Love is Kind
(1 Corinthians 13:4)

Preps

Reproduce Ice Cream Cone on page 38 on to white cardstock for each child. Punch holes in the red construction paper to make red confetti and place in the resealable plastic bag. Create a sample craft for children to view.

E-Z Steps

1. Hold up sample craft. Tell children to color the cone portion of their Ice Cream Cone brown.

2. Ask them what their two favorite ice cream flavors are? Have them color their ice cream scoops those flavors.

3. Instruct them to cut out their Ice Cream Cone.

4. Tell them to apply glue where indicated on their Ice Cream Cone, then cover the glue with the red confetti until the cherry is completely covered.

5. Hand each child about five mini-sticky notes. Ask children to place notes where indicated on the Ice Cream Cone. Have them think of a friend whom they can show kindness. Print that friend's name on the first sticky note.

6. Ask the children to memorize and discuss 1 Corinthians 13:4, "Love is patient, love is kind ..."

Teachables

Who loves ice cream? What are your favorite flavors? Remark how everyone loves ice cream because it is sweet. People who do kind things for others are said to be sweet. Showing kindness to others takes practice. Encourage the children that every time they eat ice cream, they should add another friend's name to their sticky notes as a reminder to show them kindness.

Glue Confetti
Here

Place Sticky
Notes Here

Love is Kind
(1 Corinthians 13:4)

Ice Cream
Cone

Faithful

* * * * * * * * *

Memory Verse

We live by faith, not by sight
(2 Corinthians 5:7)

In Times of Trouble

Based on Genesis 40:1-23; 41:1-43

* * * * * * * * * * * * * * * * * * *

In a dark and dreary dungeon, a young innocent Hebrew prisoner named Joseph stood with gloom in his eyes as he prayed: "God, will I ever be released from Pharaoh's prison?"

Shortly before, Joseph successfully revealed the meaning of a fellow prisoner's dream with God's help. The prisoner was freed and his position restored as Pharaoh's cupbearer, just as Joseph said. The cupbearer promised to speak to the Pharaoh about Joseph's release, but as time passed, *no cupbearer, no Pharaoh, no release!* Joseph's chin dropped as doubt set in.

God, knowing all things and having favor on Joseph was about to create a vision in the Pharaoh's mind that would change Joseph's life. God called upon our brown, four-legged presence to help create this vision. We grazed and ate reeds of tall grass near the Nile River where the Pharaoh stood. Our sight, and *moo moo* sounds, annoyed the Pharaoh and sent him inside for a nap, but our brown, four-legged vision stayed. *Can you guess what animal we are yet? [pause]*

Pharaoh's dream began with seven chubby cows coming up from the Nile River, followed by seven skinny cows. *"Whoa!* Did you see that?" I asked my cow friends. "Those skinny-minis gobbled up those chubby cows. *Whew! Thank God this is only a dream."* The Pharaoh, troubled by what he saw, jolted upright but fell fast asleep again. The second dream was more disturbing: seven unhealthy grains swallowed up seven healthy grains and the Pharaoh awoke.

No magician or wise man in all of Pharaoh's palace could interpret the Pharaoh's dreams. The cupbearer suddenly appeared before the Pharaoh and shouted, "I know a prisoner named Joseph, who *slam-dunked* the interpretation of my dream!" The Pharaoh quickly ordered Joseph's release and asked, "Joseph, can you interpret dreams?" Joseph, realizing God's hand was in his release, restored his faith and confidently replied, *"I cannot, but God can!"* Joseph began revealing Pharaoh's dreams with God's help. "Your dreams are one and the same. The chubby cows and healthy grains mean seven years of abundant food for your Egyptian people. The skinny cows and unhealthy grains that follow mean seven years of famine." "No food?" Pharaoh asked. "Yes, and God will allow this to happen soon." The Pharaoh rewarded Joseph to the position of second-in-command, in charge of preparing for the famine. Joseph learned that, *in times of trouble, have faith!* Know God is always with you and will bring things around for your good.

Can You Guess The Answer?

    1. What did Joseph learn about faith during his time of trouble?

    2. How can you show faith in your times of trouble?

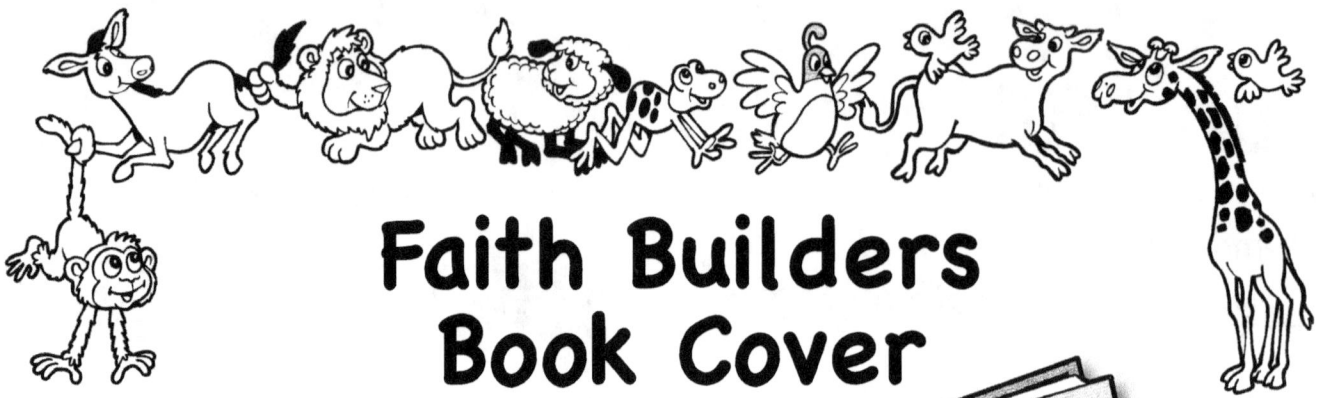

Faith Builders
Book Cover

Supplies

colored cardstock
email/phone nos. of children's
    parents
student's Bible
extra Bibles
20" x 30" Christian-style
  gift-wrap sheets
scissors, clear tape

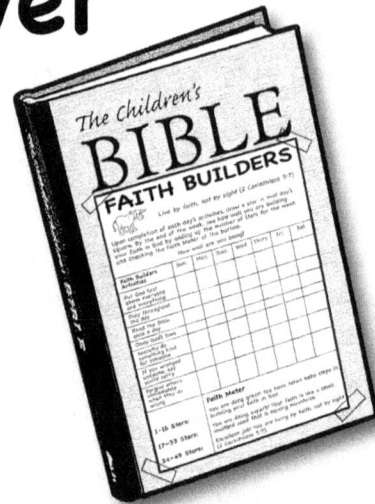

Preps

Reproduce Faith Builders Chart on page 41 on to colored cardstock, two per child. E-mail or call children's parents to remind them to ask their children to bring their Bible to class for the Faith Builders Class Project. If possible, bring extra Bibles for those children who do not have a Bible. Create a sample craft for children to view.

E-Z Steps

1. Hold up sample craft. Tell children they will create a book cover for their Bible.

2. Give out one gift-wrap sheet per child. Ask them to lay open their Bible on to the backside of the gift-wrap sheet. Show them how to cover their Bible, cutting off excess where needed and securing the corners with clear tape.

3. Instruct them to cut around the border of their Faith Builders Chart and tape to the front of their Bible. Let the children read aloud each Faith Builder activity from their chart.

4. Ask the children to memorize 2 Corinthians 5:7, "We live by faith, not by sight."

Teachables

Suggest the children begin living by faith, not by sight. Ask them to do Faith Builder Activities daily from their Faith Builders Chart. As they complete each activity daily, tell them to draw a star next to that activity. At the end of the week, tell them to count up the number of stars. By using the Faith Meter, tell them this is their way to see how well they are doing. Encourage and challenge the children to see how many activities they can complete before next week's class. Hand out an extra copy of the Faith Builders Chart for the children to take home to make additional copies for future weeks.

FAITH BUILDERS

Live by faith, not by sight (2 Corinthians 5:7)

Upon completion of each day's activities, draw a star in that day's square. By the end of the week, see how well you are building your faith in God by adding up the number of stars for the week and checking the Faith Meter at the bottom.

How well are you doing?

Faith Builders Activities	Sun.	Mon.	Tues.	Wed.	Thurs.	Fri.	Sat.
Put God first above everyone and everything							
Pray throughout the day							
Read the Bible once a day							
Obey God's laws							
Secretly do something kind for someone							
If you wronged someone, say you're sorry							
Forgive others immediately when they do wrong							

Faith Meter

1–16 Stars: You are doing great! You have taken baby steps in building your faith in God.

17–33 Stars: You are doing superb! Your faith is like a small mustard seed that is moving mountains.

34–49 Stars: Excellent job! You are living by faith, not by sight (2 Corinthians 5:7).

Faith Builders Chart

Store n' Share Tracts

Supplies

scissors, pencil
colored craft foam
hole punch
20" plastic colored cord
multi-colored beads, seven per child
stick-on fasteners
self-adhesive craft foam cutouts
   (*e.g.* crosses, flowers)
self-adhesive craft foam letters
  that spell FAITH, one per child
Jesus tracts

Preps

Reproduce Tract Pouch on page 43 for each child. Cut out the Tract Pouch outline. Trace the outline of the Tract Pouch and the hole locations on to the colored craft foam, one per child. Using the hole punch, punch the hole locations where indicated. Create a sample craft for children to view.

E-Z Steps

1. Hold up sample craft. Ask children to fold their craft foam Tract Pouch in half and line-up the holes. Tell them to insert one end of the plastic cord through the first hole nearest the top flap and knot tie several times.

2. Instruct them to insert one multi-color bead on to the plastic cord, looping the cord through the next hole, and continue looping and adding beads for every other opening and lastly, knot-tie the cord at the bottom of the Tract Pouch.

3. Show where to place each stick-on fastener so the Tract Pouch flap closes properly.

4. Suggest they decorate their Tract Pouch: (flap side) with craft foam cutouts and (backside) with FAITH craft foam letters diagonally and print 2 Cor. 5:7 near the bottom.

Teachables

Ask children why we should share our faith in Jesus with others. Give out several Jesus tracts to each child to store in their Tract Pouch. Suggest they give out a tract to someone who sounds interested in knowing more about Jesus.

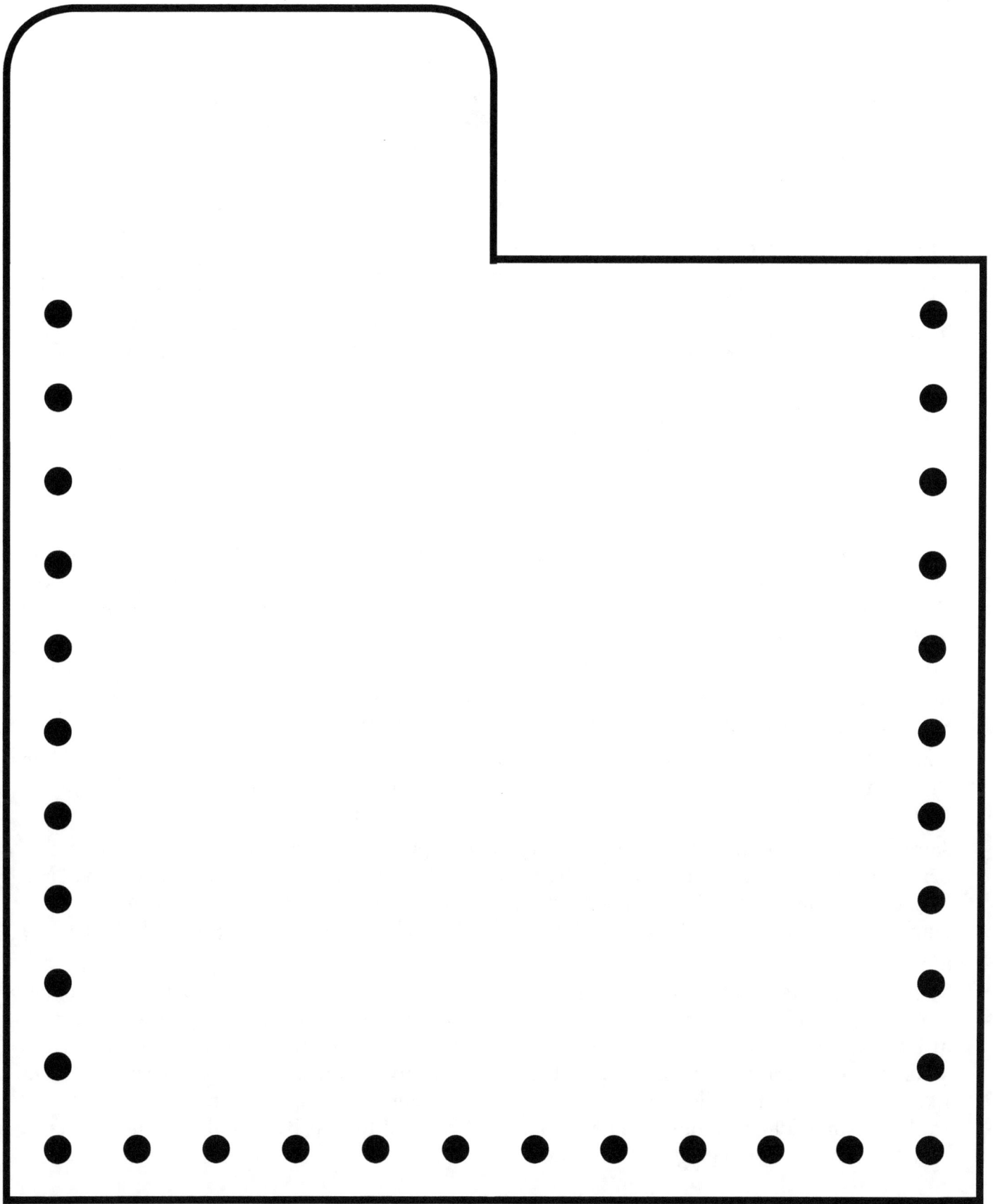

Tract Pouch

43

Bold

* * * * *

Memory Verse

The Lord is with me; he is my helper.
I will look in triumph on my enemies
(Psalm 118:7)

Mr. Slithery, at Your Service!

Based on Exodus 7:1-13

* * * * * * * * * * * * * *

What's that I hear? Voices? I poked my head high into the air to allow the sound waves to absorb into my skin down to my inner ear. With my long and scaly body, I wiggled and slithered closer to hear. It's God's voice saying, "Moses! The Egyptian king Pharaoh is holding my people, the Israelites as slaves. With Aaron as your prophet, visit the Pharaoh and perform miraculous signs in my name. Show the Pharaoh that *I am the one and only living God!* Instruct Aaron to tell the Pharaoh to let my people go. The Pharaoh will not listen as I will harden his heart for now. But once I free the Israelites, I will stretch my hand over Egypt with a mighty judgment and the Egyptians will know, without a doubt, *I am the one and only living God.*"

Moses and Aaron obeyed God and left for Pharaoh's palace. Meanwhile, God appeared to me and said, "I need your help to boldly partake in a miracle that will take place soon." Speechless, yet excited, I shook my head yes and eagerly awaited.

Once Moses and Aaron approached the Pharaoh's palace, God commanded Moses, "When Pharaoh says to you 'Perform a miracle,' instruct Aaron to throw down his staff before the Pharaoh." And Aaron did just that. And guess what happened?

Aaron's long, wooden staff miraculously became slippery, slithery me. Here's my chance to bring you glory, Lord. With the spotlight on me, I looked up at Moses, as if to say, "Mr. Slithery, at your Service." Moses nodded a sign to begin. Fearlessly, I curled my long, strong, leathery body around the Pharaoh's leg and boldly tightened. *Can you guess what animal I am yet? [pause]*

The prideful Pharaoh didn't even flinch! He just tried to stomp my snake head with his foot. Uncoiling quickly, I showed my fangs and wagged my rattle of a tail at him, ready to strike at any moment. The Pharaoh just ordered wise men and sorcerers to turn their staffs into snakes. I was surrounded. Looking with triumph on my enemies, I opened my rubber band-like jaws wide and swallowed them whole. What a jaw-dropping moment! But just as God said, the smug Pharaoh hardened his heart and refused to free His people. Even so, what a privilege Lord to bring glory to your name!

Can You Guess The Answer?

1. What did the snake boldly do to bring God glory against the Pharaoh?
2. How bold are you? Do you bring glory to God when someone speaks against God?

44

Be Bold!
Share Christer

The Lord is with me; he is my helper. I will look in triumph on my enemies.
Psalm 118:7

When I called you answered me; you made me bold and stouthearted.
Psalm 138:3

I can do everything through him who gives me strength.
Philippians 4:13

Supplies

colored cardstock
chenille stem
Bible
pencil
scissors
hole punch

Preps

Reproduce Snake on page 46 on to colored cardstock for each child. Cut the chenille stem into 3" pieces for each child. **[For younger children, may want to print the verses on Body Part Nos. 1, 2 and 3 before the children begin.]** Create a sample craft for children to view.

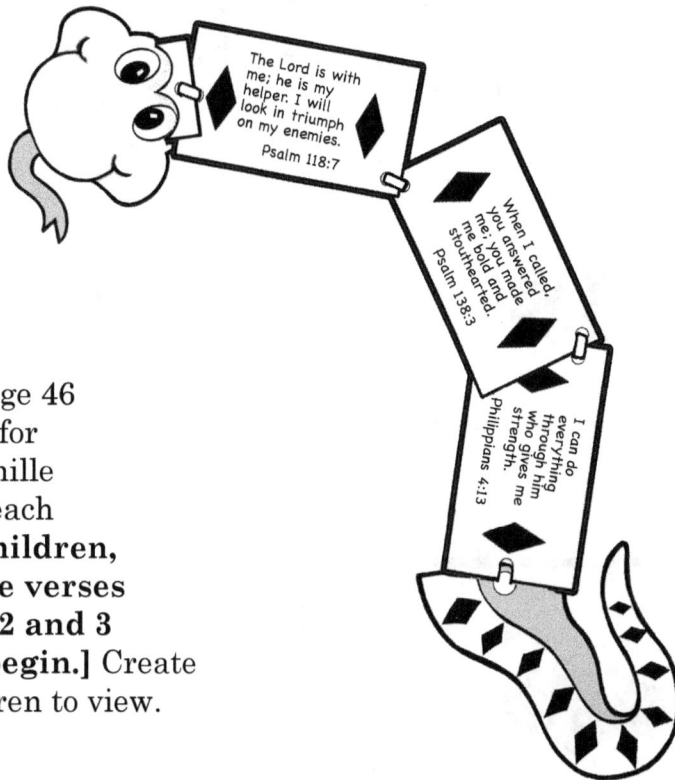

E-Z Steps

1. Ask the children to open their Bible to look up the Bible verses located on each Snake Body Part Nos. 1, 2 and 3. Instruct them to print each verse on the appropriate lines provided.

2. Tell them to cut out the Head, Tail and Body Part Nos. 1, 2 and 3.

3. Tell children to hole punch each circle located on the Head, Tail and Body Part Nos. 1, 2 and 3.

4. Hold up sample craft. Insert one end of a 3" chenille stem into the opening on the Snake's Head and the other end into the center opening of Body Part No. 1 (Psalm 118:7). **Loosely** twist tie chenille stem to allow movement of snake parts. Do the same to connect Psalm 118:7 to Psalm 138:3 (Body Part No. 2); Psalm 138:3 with Philippians 4:13 (Body Part No. 3) and Philippians 4:13 with the Snake's Tail.

Teachables

Suggest the children tape their curvy snake to a special place at home (*e.g.* bedroom dresser mirror). Encourage them to memorize one Bible verse each day about being bold so they will be ready to share Christ with others.

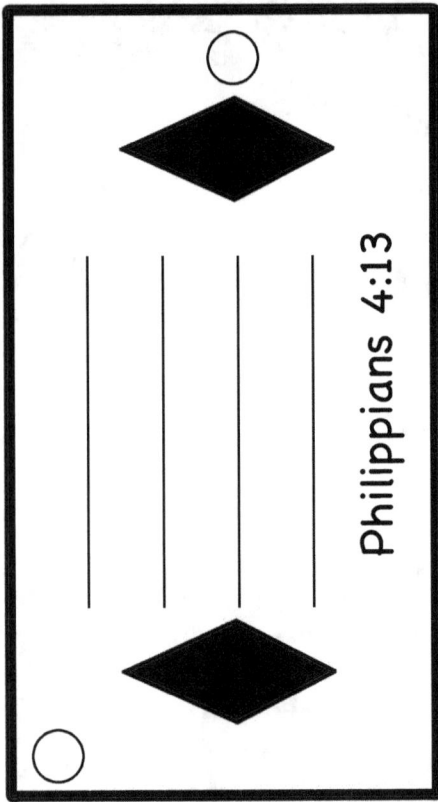

3

Philippians 4:13

Body
Parts

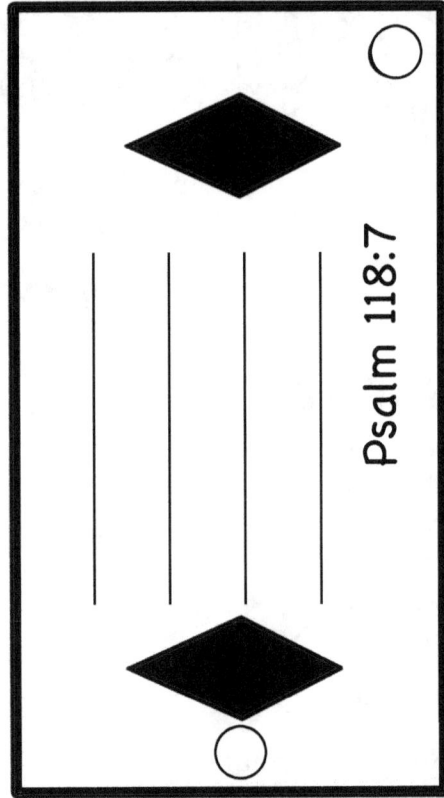

1

Psalm 118:7

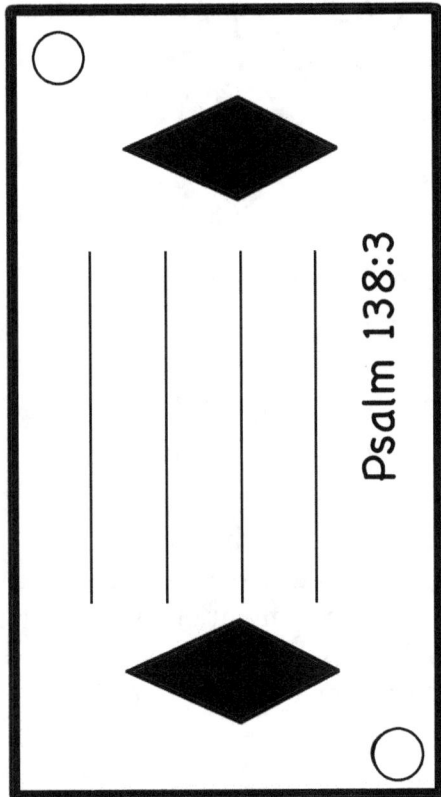

2

Psalm 138:3

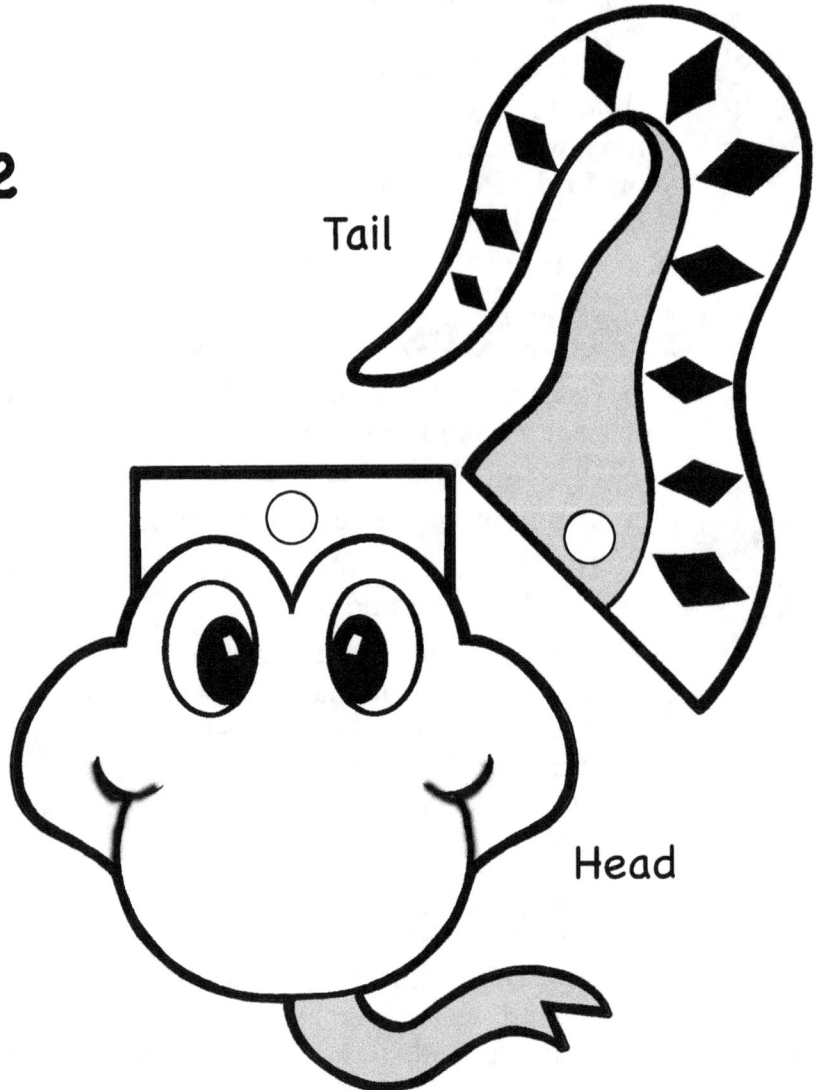

Tail

Head

Snake

Optical Illusion Megaphone

Supplies

white cardstock
crayons
scissors
stapler
black permanent marker

Preps

Reproduce the Megaphone on page 48 on to white cardstock for each child. Create a sample craft for children to view.

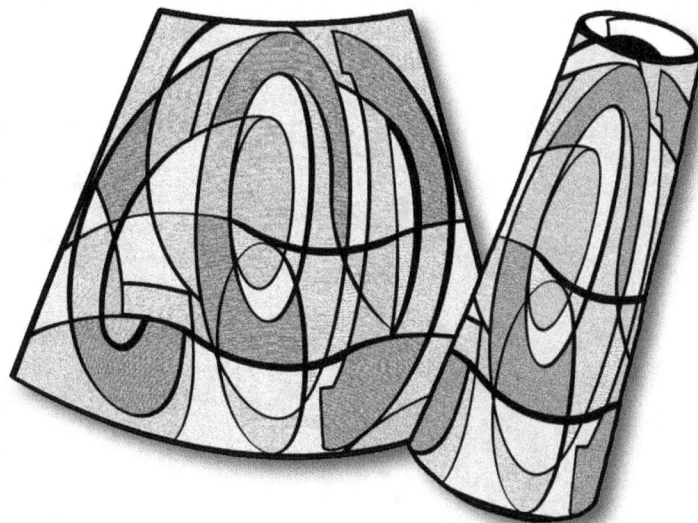

E-Z Steps

1. Ask the children to choose four to six different crayon colors.

2. Hold up sample craft. Tell them that they will color in every enclosed area or shape on their Megaphone using only those four to six crayons selected. Instruct them **not** to color any 2 side-by-side enclosed areas or shapes using the same color (this will create an optical illusion).

3. Tell them to cut out their Megaphone.

4. Help the children join the Megaphone ends together (see illustration above) and staple to secure. Ask children to look up, memorize and print John 3:16 on their Megaphone using a permanent marker.

Teachables

Encourage the children to share their faith in Christ with others. Offer this suggestion: Create a Bible Games Day at your home (*e.g.*, games they may play in Sunday school class). Tell them to invite friends who may not know Christ. Serve food and drink. Suggest they use their megaphone to referee the Bible games. Here's your chance to be bold for Christ!

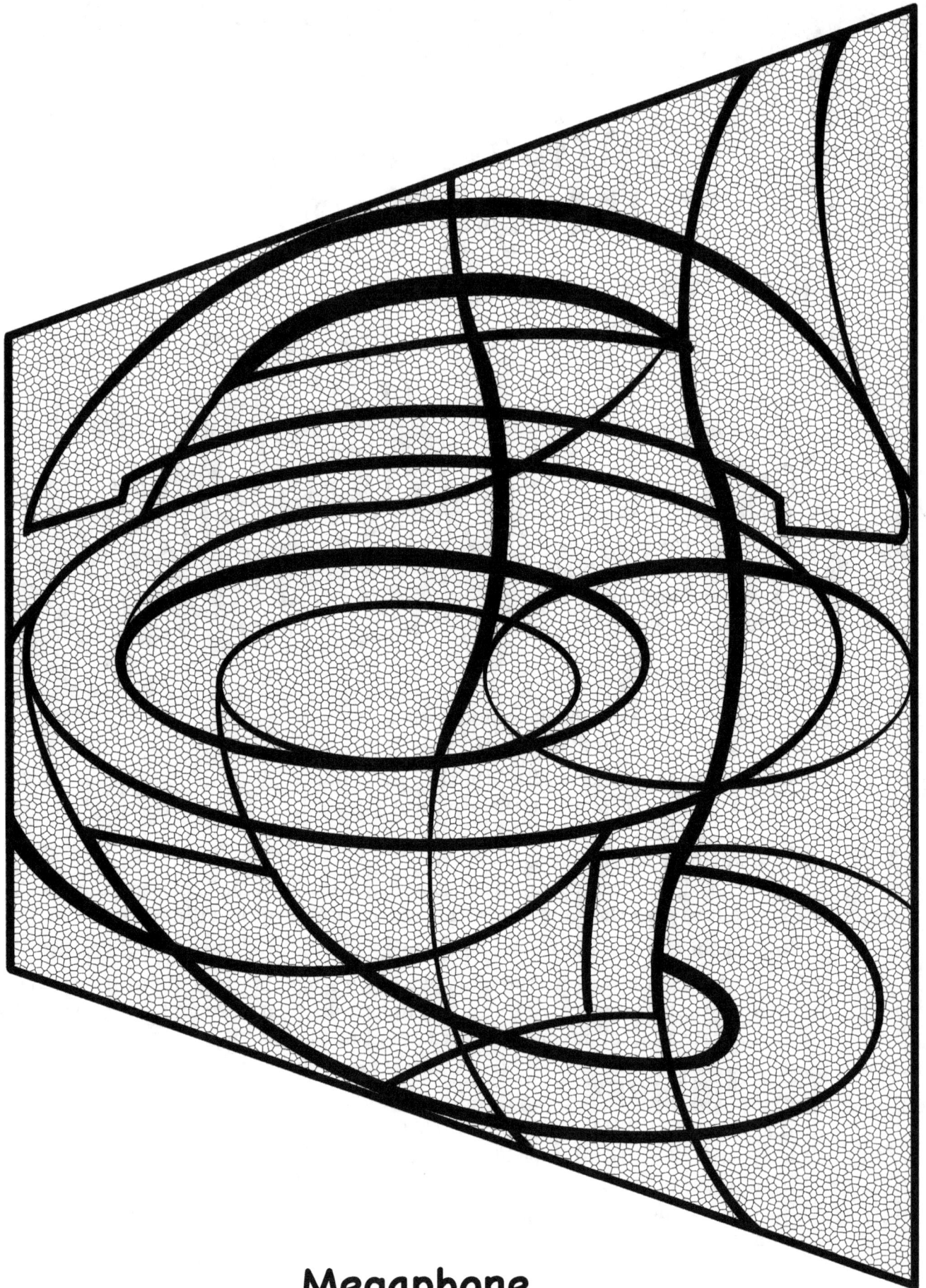

Megaphone

Joyful

* * * * * * *

Memory Verse

Worship the Lord with gladness; come before him with joyful songs **(Psalm 100:2)**

Ready for Action!
Based on Exodus 7:25-8:15
* * * * * * * * * * * * * * * * *

"Pass the suntan lotion," I said, as we sunned ourselves on the lily pads floating in the Nile River. Patiently, we wait for a sign from the Lord. "Are you ready to hop into action?" I asked the others. The sun tanners showed their readiness by filling their balloon-like vocal sacs with sweet air and bursting into praise songs to the Lord. *"Joyful, joyful, we adore thee!"*

Seven days passed since the last plague or curse on the Pharaoh, the king of Egypt. The stubborn Pharaoh refused to let the Lord's people go. The Lord called upon our help with the next plague.

The plague began when the Lord sent Moses and Aaron to visit the Pharaoh with this message: "Let my people go, so that they may worship me. If you refuse to let them go, I will plague your whole country." We hopped to attention! The Pharaoh only laughed at us. Moses told Aaron to stretch out his staff over the water. *Woo hoo! Hippity Hop!* That's our sign to do our thing. We jumped off our lily pads into the Nile River in record numbers. Using our short front legs, long hind legs and web-like feet, we swam over to the Pharaoh's palace. We hopped up onto the palace floor and leaped great distances into palace ovens, palace bedrooms and onto palace beds. We were all over the place! We even landed on the Pharaoh and his officials with our slimy selves. The whole country was covered with wet, slimy, spotty green web-like creatures. *Can you guess what animal we are yet? [pause]*

Surprisingly, as the Pharaoh turned his head, he found me sitting on his shoulder. With my bulging eyes, I winked lovingly. With my huge mouth, I cracked a joyful smile. The Pharaoh just shooed me away with his prideful self. He tried to match the Lord's power by instructing his magicians to bring on more frogs. Frogs were everywhere, with no relief in sight! The plague was finally too much for him to bear. The Pharaoh asked Moses to pray to the Lord to take away the pesky frogs. He promised that he would then, let the Lord's people go. Moses agreed and left the palace to pray. The Lord heard Moses' prayer. He agreed to keep the frogs floating in the Nile River, but removed the ones on land. Sensing relief, the Pharaoh only hardened his heart and refused to let the people go.

We continued singing joyful praises to the Lord because we knew, even for a short time, we helped to humble the Pharaoh's heart. It won't be long now Pharaoh before you let the Lord's people go!

Can You Guess The Answer?
1. The frogs were waiting for a sign from the Lord. What was that sign?
2. What can we do to show our joy for Christ to others?

Hippity Hoppity Door Hanger

Supplies

bright colored cardstock
green cardstock
scissors
glue
cotton balls, two per child

Preps

Reproduce the Door Hanger on page 51 on to bright colored cardstock and the Frog Parts on page 52 on to green cardstock for each child. Reproduce the Bible story, *Ready for Action!* on page 49. Create a sample craft for children to view.

DO GOD'S WORK

Psalm 100:2

E-Z Steps

1. Assist children in cutting out their Door Hanger and Frog Parts (For young children or children with special needs, suggest they cut the legs of their Frog Body using the dashed lines).

2. Hold up sample craft. Suggest they apply glue to a cotton ball then place where indicated on the Frog Body. Next, have them glue the Frog Head to the top of that cotton ball.

3. Ask children to glue the second cotton ball to the Door Hanger, where indicated with an asterisk. Next, have them glue the Frog Body to top of that cotton ball (frog's head should face downward as if he is jumping off the Door Hanger). Allow time for craft to dry.

4. Read Psalm 100:2 Bible verse from the Bible story page and have them repeat.

Teachables

Encourage children to hang their Hippity Hoppity Door Hanger (*e.g.* around their bedroom door handle) as a reminder for them to do God's work with a joyful smile!

DO GOD'S WORK

*

Psalm 100:2

Door Hanger

51

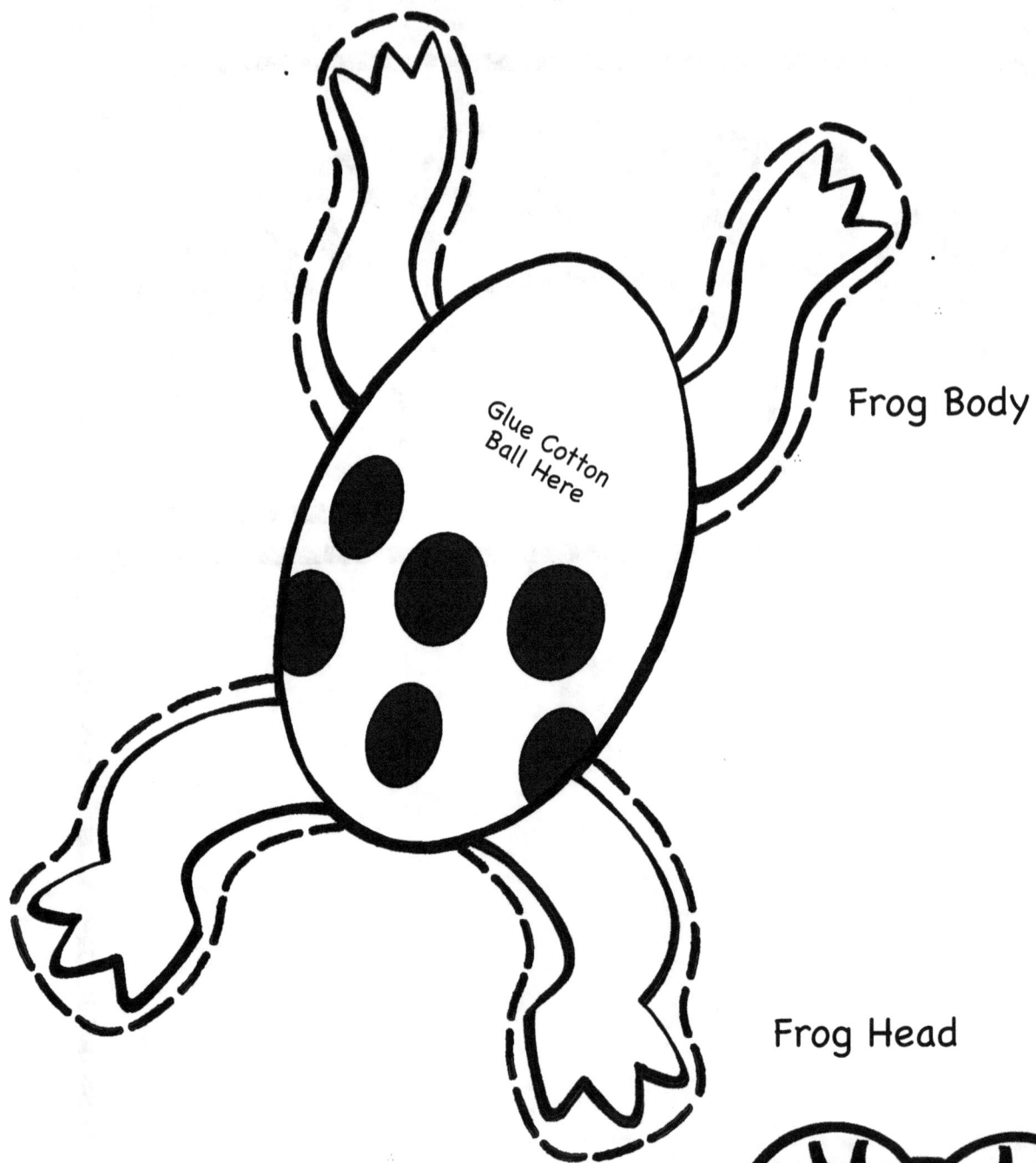

Glue Cotton Ball Here

Frog Body

Frog Head

Frog Parts

Blooming Joy
Recipe Cardholder

Supplies

colored cardstock
clay ball
baby food jar
scissors
colored chenille stems,
    three per child
clear tape
clear plastic fork

Cutzie Sugar Cookies

2/3 cup butter   1 egg
3/4 cup sugar   4 tspns milk
1 tspn vanilla   2 cups sifted all-purpose flour
     1 1/2 tspns baking powder

Cream butter, sugar and vanilla well. Add egg to creamed mixture. Beat dough until fluffy. Stir in milk. Mix dry ingredients together and blend into creamed mixture. Cut dough in half and chill for a hour.

Roll out first half of dough onto a floured surface to 1/8 inch thickness. Using cutzie shapes, cut out shapes and place on greased cookie sheet. Do same for second half of dough. Bake at 375 degrees: 6 to 8 minutes.

Worship the Lord with gladness; come before Him with joyful songs (Psalm 100:2)

Serve
The Lord
With Gladness

Preps

Reproduce Flower Pots,
Flowers, and Recipe Card
on pages 54 and 55 on to
colored cardstock for each child.
Place a clay ball into the bottom
of each baby food jar, one per child.
Create a sample craft for children to view.

E-Z Steps

1. Ask children to cut out their Flower Pots, Flowers and Recipe Card.

2. Hold up sample craft. Let them choose three of their favorite chenille stem colors. Have them twirl each chenille stem around their finger for a curly effect. Tell them to tape a flower to one end of each chenille stem. Insert the other ends of the chenille stems into the clay ball.

3. Instruct them to insert the handle side of the clear fork into the clay ball, behind the flowers.

4. Suggest they read the Bible verse on their Recipe Card, Psalm 100:2 before inserting into the prongs of the plastic fork.

5. Inform children to glue the Serve the Lord with Gladness Flower Pot to the front of the baby food jar and the other Flower Pot to the back of the baby food jar. Allow time for craft to dry.

Teachables

Psalms 100:2 says to Serve the Lord with Gladness. Bake *Cutzie Sugar Cookies* and Serve the Lord with Gladness by sharing your cookies with a sick elderly neighbor or needy church person.

Serve
The Lord
With Gladness

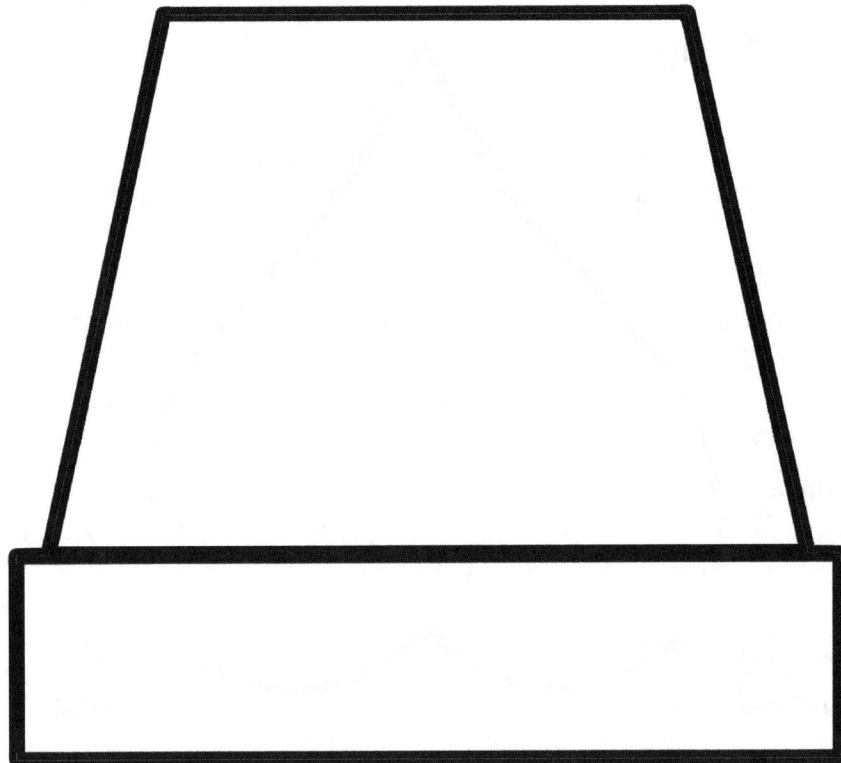

Flower Pots

Flowers

Cutzie Sugar Cookies

2/3 cup butter	1 egg
3/4 cup sugar	4 tspns milk
1 tspn vanilla	2 cups sifted all-purpose flour
	1 1/2 tspns baking powder

Cream butter, sugar and vanilla well. Add egg to creamed mixture. Beat dough until fluffy. Stir in milk. Mix dry ingredients together and blend into creamed mixture. Cut dough in half and chill for an hour.

Roll out first half of dough onto a floured surface to 1/8 inch thickness. Using cutzie shapes, cut out shapes and place on greased cookie sheet. Do same for second half of dough. Bake at 375 degrees: 6 to 8 minutes.

Worship the Lord with gladness; come before Him with joyful songs (Psalm 100:2)

Recipe Card

Responsible

* * * * * * * * * * * * * *

Memory Verse

Whatever you do, work at it with all your heart, as working for the Lord, not for men (Colossians 3:23)

Bugs! Bug, Bug, Bug

Based on Exodus 10:1-20

* * * * * * * * * * * * *

Fluttering my wings and stretching out my hind legs, I glided in for a landing on the palace floor. My big, buggy, bulging eyes turned toward Moses and Aaron as they entered the palace of the prideful Pharaoh, the king of Egypt.

Moses cleared his throat to deliver a stern message to the Pharaoh and said, "The Lord commands that if you do not let His people worship Him, He will send another plague. This plague will devour what little is left of Egypt." As I high-jumped across the palace floor, Moses pointed to me and warned, "a swarm of these annoying bugs will bug, bug, bug you Pharaoh and, like a blanket, they will cover the land." The smug and prideful Pharaoh ignored the warning. Moses and Aaron shook their heads in disgust and left the palace.

Pharaoh's officials pleaded with the king: "Let the people go, so that they may worship the Lord their God. Do you not yet realize that Egypt is ruined?" After some thought, the Pharaoh asked Moses and Aaron to return and said, "Go worship the Lord your God, but before you do, who will be leaving?" Moses revealed, "Our young and old, our families, and our flocks and herds." "What! No way," the Pharaoh shouted. "Only men can leave to worship God" as Moses and Aaron were thrown out.

I had better alert the others to the work the Lord is depending on us to do. *Lift off!* I jumpstarted my green, grasshopper-like body off the palace floor and flew to the others. *Can you guess what animal we are yet? [pause]*

The Lord told Moses, "Stretch out your hand over Egypt." *"Focus locusts!* Here we go," I said. Just then, an east wind, commanded by the Lord, blew miles of hungry locusts into one big, black cloud that covered the land of Egypt. We swarmed the Pharaoh, his officials, and their houses. We devoured the crops in the fields and the fruits on the trees. We were maddening!

Swat! Swat! The Pharaoh became a human fly swatter. Piercing screams from the Pharaoh attracted Moses and Aaron's return pronto! The bug-ridden and humbled Pharaoh said, "Pray to the Lord your God to take this deadly plague away." Moses and Aaron agreed and high-fived as they left to pray. The Lord answered their prayer and ordered a west wind to carry us locusts away. We were happy to work for you Lord and do what we do best. *Bug, Bug, Bug!*

Can You Guess The Answer?

1. How did God depend on the locusts to humble the Pharaoh?
2. What work is God asking you to do for Him?

Learn a Verse-A-Day

> DO NOT FEAR, FOR
> I AM WITH YOU
> Isaiah 41:10

Supplies

yellow paper, glue
magnet, scissors
spring-clip wooden clothespin
yellow chenille stem
green round-slotted wooden clothespin
green chenille stem
fine-tip black marker
black sequins

Preps

Reproduce Verses on page 58 on to yellow paper for each child. Glue the magnet to a flat side of the spring-clip wooden clothespin, one per child. Allow time to dry. Bend the yellow chenille stem in half. Open the spring-clip wooden clothespin to insert the midpoint of the yellow chenille stem into the opening, then release to secure. Lay the green round-slotted wooden clothespin flat on to the non-magnet side of the spring-clip wooden clothespin (see illustration above). Twist-tie the yellow chenille stem securely joining both clothespins. Bend the green chenille stem in half then insert the midpoint into the V-portion of the spring-clip wooden clothespin. Twist-tie the green chenille stem securely joining both clothespins. Create a sample craft for children to view.

E-Z Steps

1. Ask the children to cut out the Verses.
2. Hold up sample craft. Show them how to curl the yellow chenille stem ends (Locust's Antenna) and bend back the green chenille stem ends into two upside down V's (Locust Legs).
3. Suggest they draw a smile on to the round portion of the green round-slotted wooden clothespin (Locust's Face) using the fine-tip black marker and glue two black sequins (Locust's Eyes).
4. Tell them to read each Verse then choose their favorite to read aloud. Allow time for craft to dry.
5. Tell children to insert their Verses into the spring-clip wooden clothespin opening and release to secure.

Teachables

Encourage children to place their Learn a Verse-A-Day Locust on their home refrigerator. Tell them to be responsible to Christ by memorizing a new Verse-A-Day.

LOVE IS PATIENT,
LOVE IS KIND

1 Corinthians 13:4

HATE WHAT IS
EVIL; CLING TO
WHAT IS GOOD

Romans 12:9

WE LIVE BY FAITH,
NOT BY SIGHT

2 Corinthians 5:7

IF WE CONFESS
OUR SINS, HE IS
FAITHFUL AND JUST

1 John 1:9

DO NOT FEAR, FOR
I AM WITH YOU

Isaiah 41:10

DO NOT REPAY
ANYONE EVIL
FOR EVIL

Romans 12:17

LOVE THE LORD
YOUR GOD WITH ALL
YOUR HEART

Matthew 22:37

Verses

ABC's of the Cross

Supplies

colored cardstock
craft knife
3" foam ball
sequins
empty shoe box
scissors
glue

Preps

Reproduce the Heart for
Jesus Cross on page 60
on to colored cardstock for
each child. **[SAFELY: Using
the craft knife cut the foam
ball in half, one-half per child.
Also, cut a slit into the rounded portion of the foam half. See Diagram
A, p. 60.]** Place a few handfuls of sequins in an empty shoebox. Create a sample
craft for children to view.

Cross diagram labels:
- B — Believe in Jesus
- A — Admit sin
- JESUS
- C — Confess your faith
- John 3:16

ABC's of the Cross Prayer
Dear God, I admit I have sinned. I believe Jesus is your Son and died for me. Please forgive me of my sins. I accept Jesus as my Lord and Savior. Thank you for coming into my life. Amen.

E-Z Steps

1. Instruct children to cut out their Heart for Jesus Cross.

2. Hold up sample craft. Ask them to slide their Heart for Jesus Cross through the slit in their foam half.

3. Tell them to apply glue to the rounded portion of their foam half and then show them how to sprinkle the sequins over the glue until completely covered. Allow time for craft to dry.

4. Ask children to memorize John 3:16, "For God so loved the world that he gave his one and only son, that whoever believes in him shall not perish but have eternal life."

Teachables

The locusts worked with all their heart for the Lord. Do you have that same love for Christ too? Say the ABC's of the Cross Prayer to ask Jesus into your heart. Share your new relationship with Christ with your parents or pastor. Begin working for Christ today by telling a friend the ABC's of the Cross.

B
Believe in Jesus

A Admit sin

JESUS

C Confess your faith

John 3:16

ABC's of the Cross Prayer

Dear God, I admit I have sinned. I believe Jesus is your Son and died for me. Please forgive me of my sins. I accept Jesus as my Lord and Savior. Thank you for coming into my life. Amen.

safely cut slit

Diagram A

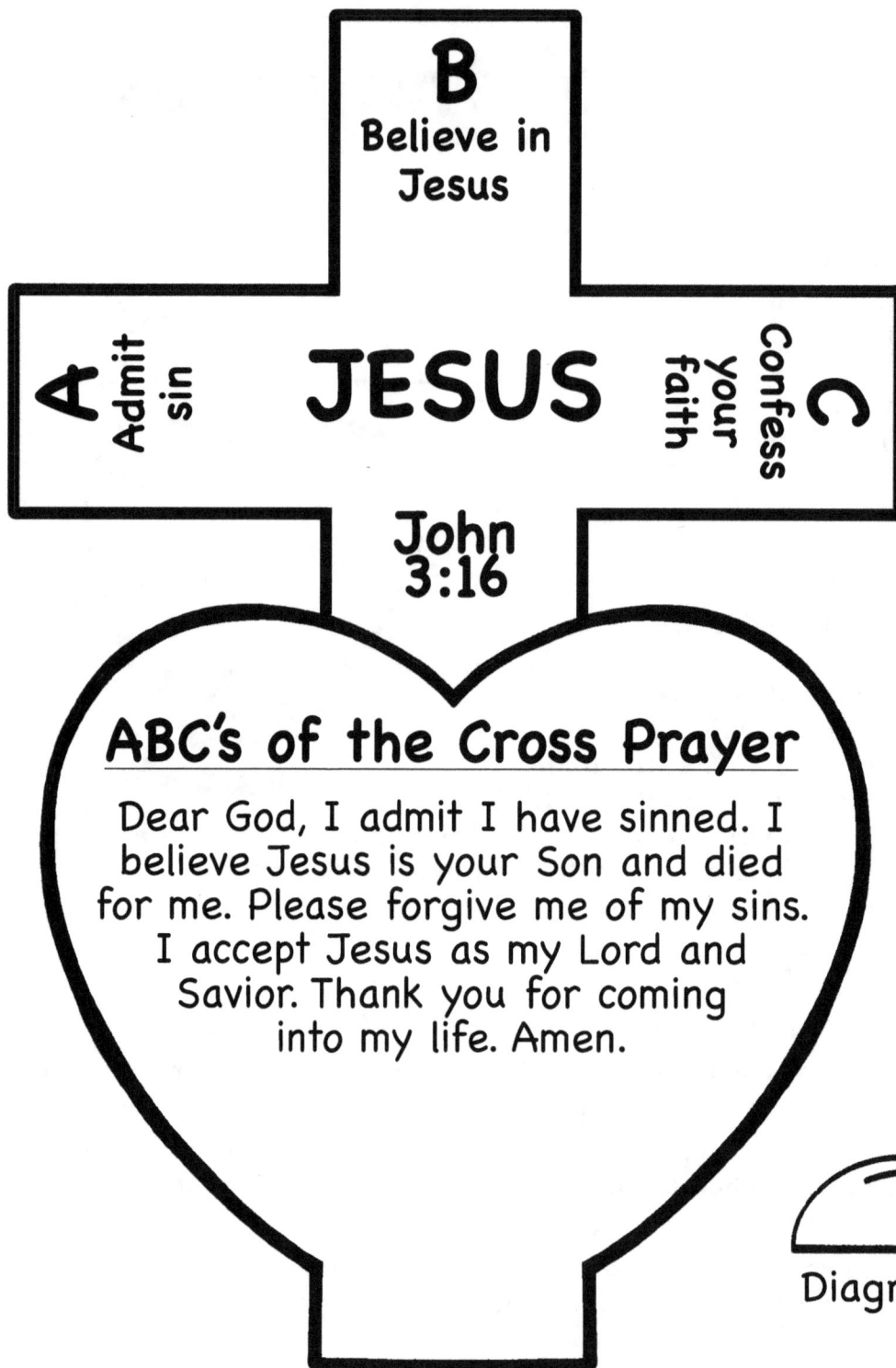

Heart for Jesus Cross

Hopeful

* * * * * * * * *

Memory Verse

Why are you downcast, O my soul? Why so disturbed within me? Put your hope in God ... **(Psalm 42:5)**

Where's My Umbrella? It's Raining!

Based on Exodus 16:1-30

* * * * * * * * * * * * *

"Ah ha! Are those red berries I see?"
I quickly shifted my wings as my small head and plump body glided in for a landing on the desert floor. My long legs and web-like feet made a firm footing into the soft sand. As soon as I began eating those luscious berries, I heard a loud *GRRRUMBLE!* "Could that be my stomach growling?" *GRRRUMBLE!* Frightened by the noise, I flew upward to a higher branch of the barberry bush for a better view. My colorful feather-like crest stood tall on my head. *Can you guess what animal I am yet? [pause]*

A large crowd of people called the Israelites appeared. They were fleeing from Egypt and Pharaoh's grips of slavery heading for the Promised Land, a new beginning. As they passed, I heard one say, "If only we had died by the Lord's hand in Egypt! There we sat around pots of meat and ate all the food we wanted, but you have brought us out into this desert to starve." They were complaining to Moses, their leader. He stopped, raised his hands to the crowd, and instructed them to set up camp.

Moses, a holy man, went off alone, and sat near the barberry bush to pray. As Moses began praying, I recognized the soft voice that spoke to Moses. It was the voice of God. The one I place my hope in, the one who provides for me daily! God told Moses He had heard His people grumble! He told Moses to tell them, "'You will know I am the Lord your God,' when I provide bread and meat for you. Place your hope in me. Gather only what you need for that day and no more." This was God's test for His people. Moses returned and shared God's instructions with the Israelites, and they waited.

In the morning, the glory of the Lord broke through the clouds, followed by a downpour. "Where's my umbrella?" I cried, "It's raining!" I quickly realized what I thought was rain was actually bread flakes called manna, falling softly and covering the camp. Most of the Israelites gathered only what they needed but others disobeyed and gathered more. God allowed their leftovers to spoil so they would learn to obey and hope in Him.

That night, God provided again. Quail appeared and covered the camp. The Israelites scrambled to catch and prepare the quail for their supper. Hey, I didn't know I was a delicacy!

God continued providing morning and night for the Israelites. On the sixth day, Moses shared God's special instructions for them: He told them to prepare enough food for two days, as the seventh day is the Sabbath, a holy day of rest. The Israelites obeyed and placed their hope in the Lord!

Can You Guess The Answer?

1. What two foods did God provide the Israelites to eat when they were hungry?
2. Name one way God provides hope for you and your family.

Home Sweet Home Bird Feeder

Supplies

yellow cardstock
bird seed
resealable plastic bag
cardboard milk carton
stapler, hole punch
scissors or craft knife
green spray paint
craft glue and craft sticks
dried lightweight leaves, twigs and acorns
9" thin twig
18" twine, string or ribbon

Preps   ***ADVANCE TIME WILL BE NEEDED***

Reproduce Pentagon Shapes and Home Sweet Home Labels on page 63 on to yellow cardstock. Separate Labels, two per child. Place bird seed in resealable plastic bag and prepare bird feeder, one per child. Wash/dry carton. Staple carton's flaps closed. Punch a center hole into the flap (see illustration above). **[SAFELY: Cut out and trace Pentagon Shapes (1½" from the bottom) to the sides of the carton with the triangles at the top. See Diagram A, p. 63.]** Under each pentagon-shaped opening, poke a center hole (¾" from the bottom). Spray paint carton exterior and let dry. Create sample craft for children to view.

E-Z Steps

1. Hold up sample craft. Show children how to apply glue and craft sticks to create a roof for their bird feeder. Apply glue to the solid sides of the bird feeder then cover with dried leaves, twigs and acorns. Allow time for craft to dry.

2. Instruct them to cut out their Home Sweet Home Labels and glue one above each pentagon-shaped opening.

3. Help them insert a twig through both bottom holes of their bird feeder.

4. Ask the children to insert twine, string or ribbon through the top hole in the flap of their bird feeder and knot tie so bird feeder can be hung up later. Print Bible verse, Psalm 42:5 on the roof.

Teachables

As we depend on God to provide food and water, birds depend on us for provisions. Encourage children to hang their Home Sweet Home Bird Feeder in their backyard. Suggest they pour bird seed into their bird feeder daily. Watch the birds enjoy!

Pentagon Shapes

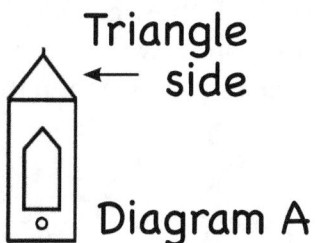

Home
Sweet
Home

Home
Sweet
Home

Home
Sweet
Home

Home
Sweet
Home

Home
Sweet
Home

Home
Sweet
Home

Home
Sweet
Home

Home
Sweet
Home

Triangle
side ←

Diagram A

Home Sweet Home Labels

Provider of Hope Suncatcher

Supplies

yellow cardstock, scissors, suction cup
7½" x 5" self-adhesive paper, two per child
different colored tissue paper scraps
hole punch, clear tape, pencil
8" yarn strips, two per child
5" yarn strips, two per child

Preps

Reproduce Cloud and Loaves of Bread on page 65 on to yellow cardstock for each child. Cut on dashed line to separate Cloud from the Loaves of Bread. Create a sample craft for children to view.

E-Z Steps

1. Ask children to cut out the Cloud, the inside of the Cloud and the three Loaves of Bread.

2. Help them peel back one self-adhesive paper, then lay down on a table with the sticky side up.

3. Hold up sample craft. Instruct them to lay the Cloud, words *Hope in the LORD* facing down, onto the center of the sticky paper. Tell them to cover the sticky portion of the center of the Cloud with different colored tissue paper scraps.

4. Help them peel back the second self-adhesive paper. With sticky side facing downward, line up with the first self-adhesive paper, press down firmly, sealing in tissue paper contents. Turn Cloud over and cut off self-adhesive paper excess from the Cloud's border.

5. Punch holes where indicated on the Cloud and Bread. Insert one end of 8" yarn through middle hole at the bottom of the Cloud, tape yarn end to the back. Insert other end of 8" yarn through hole of the middle Loaf of Bread and tape yarn to the back. Do the same for right and left holes on the Cloud using the accompanying Loaves of Bread and 5" yarns.

6. Ask children to fill in the questions on the Loaves of Bread. Lastly, have them insert the 8" yarn through the top hole on the Cloud, create a loop and knot tie. Give them a suction cup to take home to hang their suncatcher. Have children memorize Matthew 6:26, "Look at the birds of the air; they do not sow or reap or store away in barns, and yet your heavenly Father feeds them. Are you not much more valuable than they?"

Teachables

Suggest the children hang their suncatcher at home. When their friends compliment their craft, encourage them to share how God gives us HOPE and provides for all of our needs.

Hope in the LORD

MATTHEW 6:26

cut out inside

Cloud

- -

God provides for our _____?

Name one way God provides for you?

Put hope in the Lord when I am _____?

Loaves of Bread

Loyal
* * * * * *

Memory Verse

A friend loves at all times ...
(Proverbs 17:17)

Balaam Warned of Danger

Based on Numbers 22:1-35
* * * * * * * * * * * * *

In the land of Moab, King Balak saw the victorious Israelite army settling into his land and fearfully exclaimed, "Oh No! My army will soon be defeated too for the Israelites are blessed by God. If only the Israelites thought they lost God's blessing," he schemed, "I would be able to fight them and drive them away." Only one person is up for this job--Balaam the prophet, or one chosen to speak for God.

King Balak sent Moabite princes to deliver his message to Balaam. Among the crowd, I trotted curiously up to my owner Balaam and nudged him, as if to say, "Who are these dudes?" My large, long, gray ears did the wave and overheard Balak's message to hire Balaam to curse the Israelites.

"Hey dudes! You want my owner to be disloyal to God?" I thought. *HEE HAW! HEE HAW!* I back-kicked. I side-kicked. I got dizzy. Balaam calmed me down then told the princes, "I will seek God's answer and let you know." God told Balaam, "Do not go to curse my people for they are blessed." Balaam shared God's message with the princes and they left to return to Balak.

Balak sent more princes with the same message. This time armed with silver and gold. God told Balaam, "Go with them, but *do only what I tell you.*" Balaam's loyalty to God soon faded as his desire for silver and gold increased. Balaam's plan was to curse the Israelites. This made God very angry.

In the morning, Balaam saddled my smaller than horse-like body and we left to travel to Moab. Suddenly, an angel of the Lord appeared and blocked the road. I protected Balaam from the harm of the angel's raised sword by turning off into a field. Balaam could not see the angel and thought I was being stubborn so he beat me to get back on the road. *Can you guess what animal I am yet? [pause]*

The angel appeared two more times. Each time, I protected Balaam. Each time, he beat me to move forward to collect his silver and gold. Miraculously God allowed me, a donkey, to speak. "Haven't I been your long-time, loyal friend? Have I not always loved you?" Balaam said, "I thought you were making a fool of me." Unexpectedly, God opened Balaam's eyes to the angel with the raised sword. The angel said, "I have come to oppose you Balaam. If your donkey wouldn't have turned away, I certainly would have killed you." Balaam humbled with his face to the ground. He learned a valuable lesson: *Love and be loyal to God and friends at all times!*

Can You Guess The Answer?

1. What made Balaam choose to be disloyal to God and his donkey?
2. Are you loyal to your friends at all times, even when they might be having a bad day?

Loyal Friends Fold-A-Frame

Supplies

colored cardstock
white cardstock
scissors
email/phone nos. of children's parents
photograph of the child
two individual photographs of
    the child's friends
pencil
glue
tape

Preps

Reproduce the Fold-A-Frame on page 68, one copy on to colored cardstock (one per child) and several copies on to white cardstock (each oval shape when separated and cut out will become a Template, one Template per child). E-mail or call children's parents to remind the children to bring three photographs for their class project. Create a sample craft for children to view.

E-Z Steps

1. Ask children to cut around the border of their colored cardstock Fold-A-Frame.

2. Hold up Template. Show children how to place the Template over each photograph (make sure each child's face is in the middle of the Template). Tell the children to trace around the Template and then carefully cut out each photograph.

3. Suggest they glue or tape down photographs to each empty oval shape on their colored cardstock Fold-A-Frame. Allow time for craft to dry.

4. Memorize and talk about John 15:12, "My command is this: Love each other as I have loved you."

5. Instruct children to fold their Fold-A-Frame on the fold lines to stand their frame upright.

Teachables

The donkey in our Bible story protected Balaam from harm because of his love and loyalty to his friend. Keep your friends close forever by loving them as Jesus loves you!

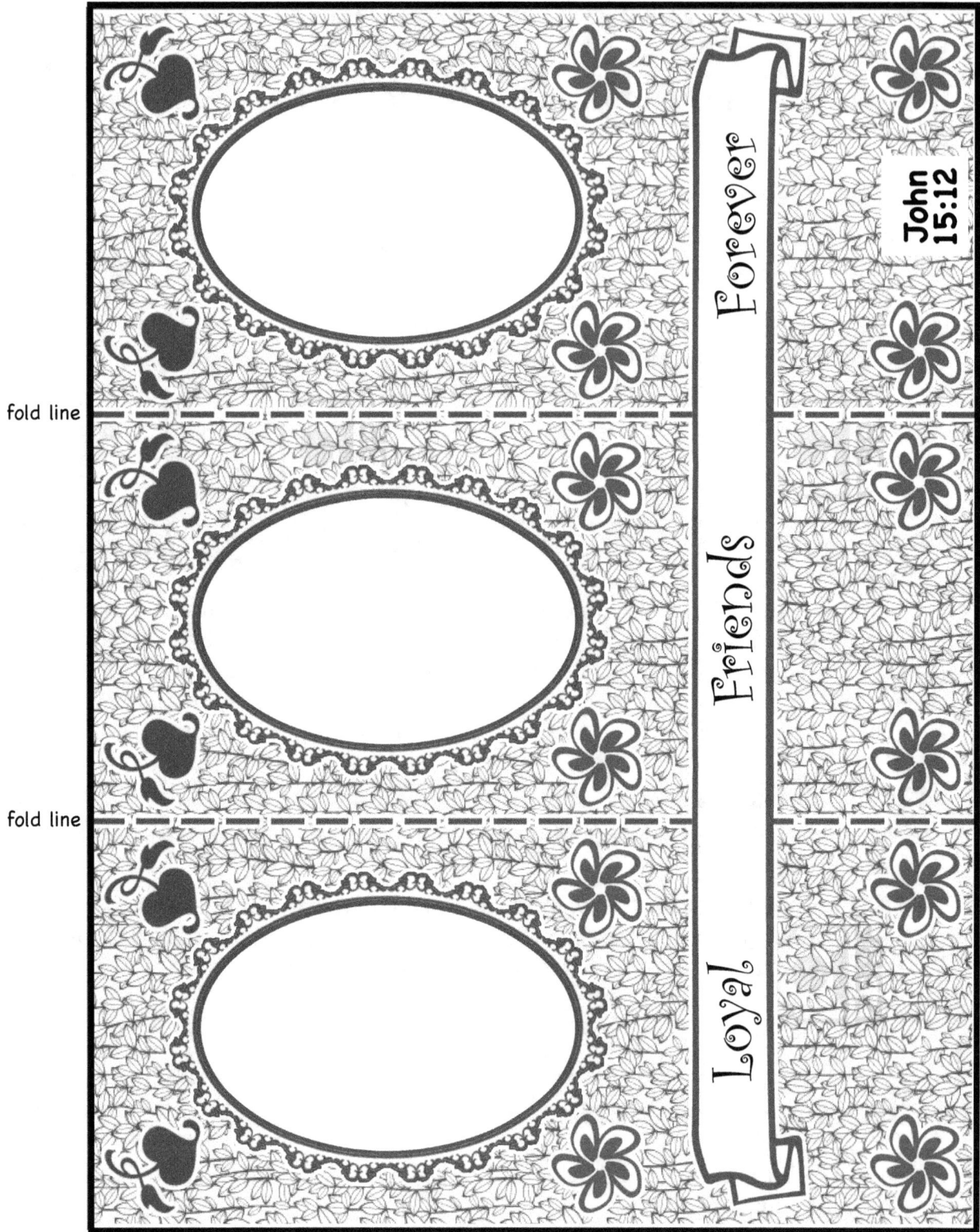

Forever

Friends

Loyal

John
15:12

fold line

fold line

Fold-A-Frame

Friendship Bracelet

Supplies

colored cardstock
36" bead cord, one per teacher
36" bead cord, one per child
tape, scissors
6 colored beads (larger openings)
hole punch

FRIENDS FOREVER
TO ___Sally___
FROM ___Donna___
Proverbs 17:17

Preps

Reproduce the Gift Tags on page 70
on to colored cardstock, one per child.
Create a sample craft for children to view.

E-Z Steps

1. Hold up bead cord to perform instructions visually for children as they create their own. Show them how to fold the cord in half. With both cord strands together, tie a knot about one-half inches down from the folded end. Securely tape the folded end to a table to prepare to bead.

2. Tell them to separate both cord strands and knot tie 8 knots in a row.

3. Ask them to slip one bead on one cord strand and knot tie to secure the bead. Continue this process of adding beads and knot tying until all remaining beads are added.

4. Instruct them to separate both cord strands and knot tie 8 knots in a row.

5. With both cord strands together, tie a knot to secure beads. From the knot, leave about 3-4 inches of cord and cut off remaining excess.

6. Ask the children to punch a hole where indicated on the Gift Tag, fill-in the To: and From: on their Gift Tag, slip the Gift Tag through both ends of the cord and knot tie several times to secure. Memorize Proverbs 17:17, "A friend loves at all times ..."

Teachables

Loyalty and friendship is everything. Do you truly love your friends as Jesus loves you? Can you be loyal to your friends even when they are having a bad day? Give your friend the friendship bracelet. Create a loyalty agreement with them: When someone gets mad, promise to never talk bad about each other, but instead talk with each other to resolve and make amends. Be loyal to your friends! Try it! You may have a lifelong friend.

FRIENDS FOREVER

TO _____

FROM _____

Proverbs 17:17

FRIENDS FOREVER

TO _____

FROM _____

Proverbs 17:17

FRIENDS FOREVER

TO _____

FROM _____

Proverbs 17:17

FRIENDS FOREVER

TO _____

FROM _____

Proverbs 17:17

FRIENDS FOREVER

TO _____

FROM _____

Proverbs 17:17

FRIENDS FOREVER

TO _____

FROM _____

Proverbs 17:17

FRIENDS FOREVER

TO _____

FROM _____

Proverbs 17:17

FRIENDS FOREVER

TO _____

FROM _____

Proverbs 17:17

Gift Tags

Resourceful

* * * * * * * * * * * * * *

Memory Verse

And my God will meet all your needs according to his glorious riches in Christ Jesus **(Philippians 4:19)**

Samson's Sweet Snack

Based on Judges 13-14
* * * * * * * * * * * * *

As the sun begins to rise, we rev up our wings and begin our day. *Buzzzz! Buzzzz!* With our long antennas, we wave goodbye to our queen. We flutter from flower to flower, sipping sweet liquid through our long, tube-like tongues. We fill our tummies full and wonder, "Where can we store our honey today?"

Returning to our queen, we were in awe of the Lord's presence and attentively listened as He asked our queen for help. "For forty years, the Israelites have been prisoners of the Philistines. It is time my people are free! I have chosen Samson, a young Nazirite, for the job. Samson has begun building mistrust with the Philistines by falling in love with one of their women. Now here is where you can help."

"A while ago, Samson walked this very pathway to the Philistine town of Timnah, when something unusual happened! Something Samson would not forget. A young, lanky lion lunged forward. With super Godly strength, Samson grabbed hold and tore the lion apart using his bare hands. All that remains now is the lion's empty carcass. Ask your workers to supply honey nearby for Samson to enjoy on his way to marry his bride."

Once the Lord departed, our queen instructed us to store our honey where Samson was sure to find! Black and gold striped insects worked non-stop, filling the largest hive-like opening they could find--the empty carcass. *Can you guess what animal we are yet? [pause]* When Samson finally appeared, he saw the honey overflowing. He hesitated, then ate and thought, *"What a sweet snack.* How resourceful of honeybees to store their honey here. *Hmmm!"*

In Timnah, while Samson attended his bridegroom feast, mistrust with the Philistines continued. Samson tested them with a riddle from his sweet snack experience, *"Out of the eater, something to eat; out of the strong, something sweet."* The puzzled Philistines became agitated. They left the feast to threaten Samson's fiancée. She later tricked Samson into giving her the answer. The confident Philistines returned to the feast with the answer to the riddle, *"What is sweeter than honey? What is stronger than a lion?"* Samson knew he was deceived! With super Godly strength, Samson slew thirty Philistines that day. This triumph was only one of many until Samson freed the Israelites.

How awesome, Lord, for Samson to use our resourcefulness in a riddle to free your people!

Can You Guess The Answer?

1. Whom did God choose to free the Israelites from the grips of the Philistines?
2. Name one way you can be resourceful like the bees.

Bee Sweet for Jesus Basket

Supplies:

yellow cardstock, hole punch
plastic baby food container
chenille stems, two per child
plastic egg (yellow if possible)
unwrapped small candies
tape, scissors, glue, felt scraps
1" black circle sticky-back craft foam
2" x ½" black sticky-back craft foam
1½" x ½" black sticky-back craft foam
fine tip black permanent marker

BEE SWEET FOR JESUS
Colossians 3:23

Preps:

Reproduce Bee Sweet Flower on page 73 on to yellow cardstock, one per child. Punch two holes, one hole on each short side under the rim of the plastic baby food container (Basket), one Basket per child. Insert one chenille stem end into the first hole and twist tie to secure. Insert the other end into the second hole and twist tie to secure. Create bee wings and antennas using the second chenille stem, one per child (see Diagram A, p. 73). Press wings/antennas together (see Diagram B, p. 73). Fill the egg with candy one-fourth full. Before closing the egg, insert the bottom of the wings/antennas into the egg opening (will be snug but will close), then tape egg closed to secure. Create a sample craft for children to view.

E-Z Steps:

1. Ask children to cut out the Bee Sweet Flower. Glue the Basket bottom where indicated on the Bee Sweet Flower. Instruct them to fill their Basket with felt scraps three-fourths full.

2. Hold up sample craft. Show them how to adhere one-inch circle craft foam to the thin end of the egg, the two-inch craft foam to the middle of the egg and the one and a half inch craft foam to the wide end of the egg, without covering up the egg's opening (see illustration above).

3. Help them spread out the bee wings and curl the bee antennas. Instruct children to draw eyes and a smile on their bee's face then lay their bee inside the Basket.

4. Have children find Colossians 3:23 in their Bible and discuss.

Teachables:

Suggest children be like the bees by thinking of creative ways to be resourceful. Be thrifty. Reuse items that might otherwise be thrown away and remember, always Bee Sweet for Jesus!

SWEET

BEE

FOR

Glue
Basket
Bottom
Here

JESUS

Colossians 3:23

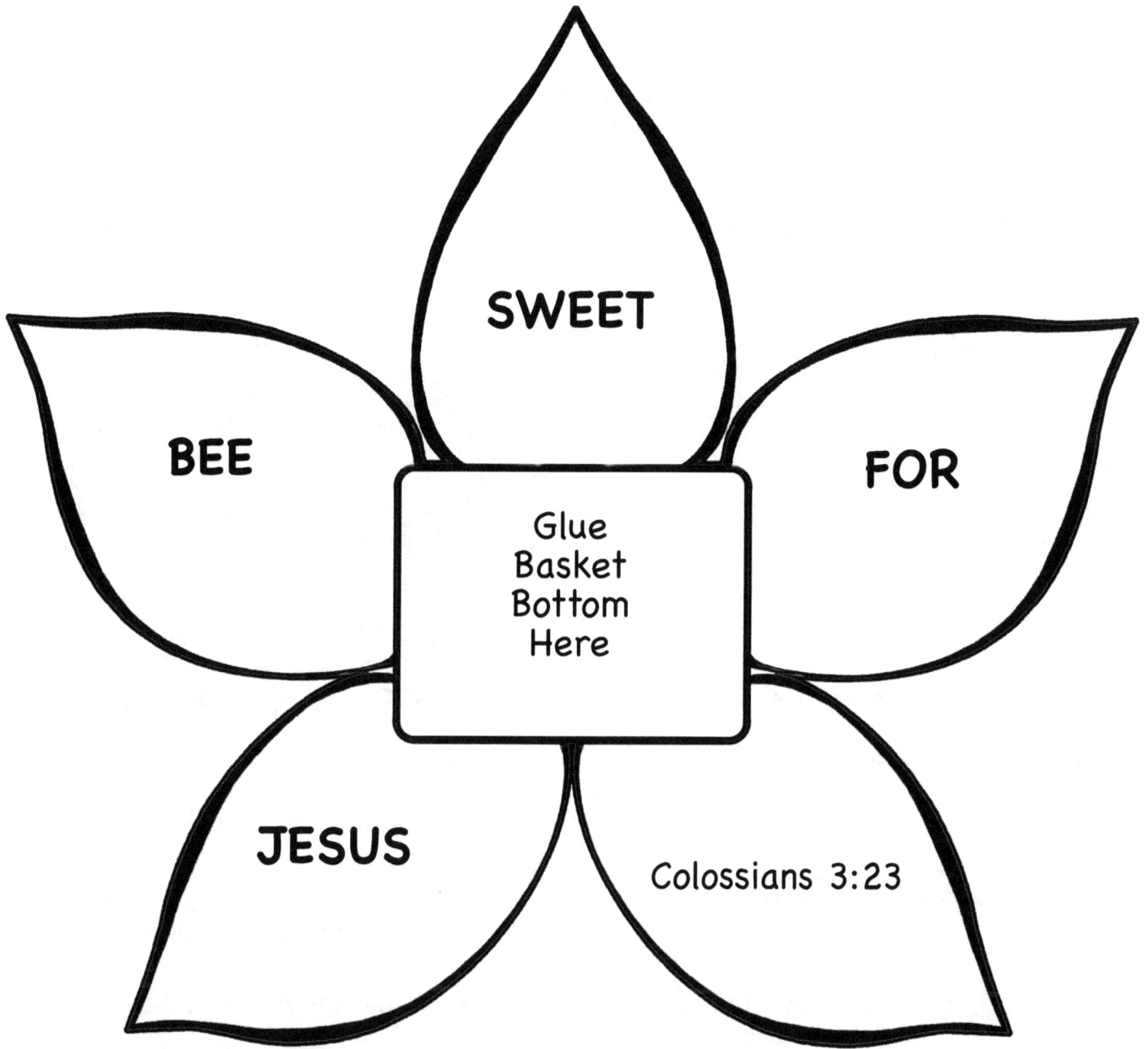

Create Bee Wings and Antennas

3. Twist
antennas
upward.
Press
together
at b.

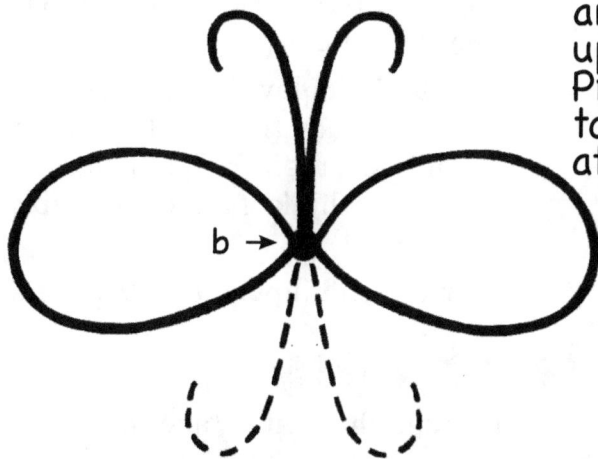

1. Bend
chenille
wire

a

2. Bend a
down to
b and
hold at b

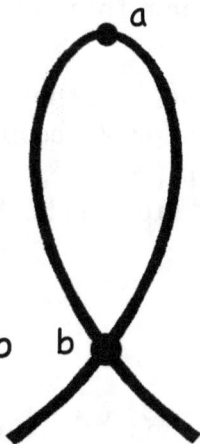

b

b →

Diagram A

Diagram B

Bee Sweet Flower

Go Green Game

Supplies

shoebox
colored wrapping paper
scissors
tape
Recyclable Items 1-6 (for example):
(1) ball of aluminum foil
(2) chenille stem
(3) plastic cup
(4) wooden clothespin
(5) felt scrap
(6) popsicle stick

Preps

Reproduce Game Instructions on page 75 for each child. Separate each Go Green Game Instruction, one per child. Create a sample craft for children to view.

E-Z Steps

1. Instruct children to wrap their shoebox with wrapping paper, bottom and lid separately, and secure with tape.

2. Ask them to cut out and tape the Go Green Game Instructions to the inside lid of their shoebox.

3. Tell them to place the Recyclable Items 1-6 inside their shoebox (*e.g.*, ball of aluminum foil, chenille stem, plastic cup, wooden clothespin, felt scrap, popsicle stick). Ask them to be resourceful – let them think of other uses for recyclable items.

4. Let children play the Go Green Game with a friend. Tell them to ask their friend to study the recyclable items inside the box for 30 seconds then close the lid. Ask their friend to name as many items as possible. Suggest children remove or think of more recyclable object(s) to add to the shoebox and then play again!

5. Memorize Philippians 4:19 and practice.

Teachables

Encourage children to take their Go Green Game home to play with their neighborhood friends. Remind children to think of resourceful ways or ways to save money by reusing items God has given them.

GO GREEN
Game Instructions

And my God will meet all your needs according to his glorious riches in Christ Jesus (Philippians 4:19)

Help friends be resourceful! Play Go Green Game. Place recyclable items inside the shoebox (*e.g.,* ball of aluminum foil, chenille stem, plastic cup, wooden clothespin, felt scrap or popsicle stick). Ask friend to study the recyclable items for 30 seconds. Close lid. Ask them to name as many recyclable items as possible. Remove/add object(s). Play again.

GO GREEN
Game Instructions

And my God will meet all your needs according to his glorious riches in Christ Jesus (Philippians 4:19)

Help friends be resourceful! Play Go Green Game. Place recyclable items inside the shoebox (*e.g.,* ball of aluminum foil, chenille stem, plastic cup, wooden clothespin, felt scrap or popsicle stick). Ask friend to study the recyclable items for 30 seconds. Close lid. Ask them to name as many recyclable items as possible. Remove/add object(s). Play again.

GO GREEN
Game Instructions

And my God will meet all your needs according to his glorious riches in Christ Jesus (Philippians 4:19)

Help friends be resourceful! Play Go Green Game. Place recyclable items inside the shoebox (*e.g.,* ball of aluminum foil, chenille stem, plastic cup, wooden clothespin, felt scrap or popsicle stick). Ask friend to study the recyclable items for 30 seconds. Close lid. Ask them to name as many recyclable items as possible. Remove/add object(s). Play again.

Game Instructions

Hospitable

* * * * * * * * * * *

Memory Verse

Share with God's people who are in need.
Practice hospitality (Romans 12:13)

Food Provided to Elijah

Based on I Kings 16:29–17:6
* * * * * * * * * * * * * * *

Attention please! Attention please! Welcome Crow family to our annual family picnic.

"Get in line," the referee screeched. "It's time for the picnic games." Sleek black crow-like birds flew beak to beak to get in line for their turn. "Who can perform the best aerial stunt this year?" the referee crowed. "Who can spread their wings and glide the farthest?" I was first in line to perform my famous double twirl backwards flip. I thought, for sure, I would hear applause. But, as I looked below, my family was preoccupied. As I flew closer, I heard the voice of God sharing a special request with them: "Soon, you will be visited by a guest. *Be hospitable and provide food for him during his stay.* Use your fine hunting skills to find bread and meat to serve him each morning and night." *Can you guess what animal we are yet? [pause]*

God asked that I come and meet our soon-to-be guest, Elijah, the prophet. "This is Mr. Crow, Elijah. He will be assisting you later. As for now, I need your help in delivering a message to Ahab, the new King of Israel. He has become very wicked and has done more evil in my eyes than any other king before him. Recently King Ahab married Jezebel, the daughter of Ethbaal, who worships the false god of Baal. King Ahab has now begun to worship Baal too and is turning my people away from me."

"Go Elijah," God said. "Deliver this message to King Ahab: 'As the Lord, the God of Israel, lives, whom I serve, there will be neither dew nor rain in the next few years except at my word.' Once you deliver the message, leave immediately, as you will be in danger. Hide in the Kerith Ravine, east of the Jordan. Mr. Crow and his family of ravens will feed you there."

Elijah left and delivered the message to King Ahab that God is the one true God. *STOMP! STOMP!* King Ahab was so angry, he stomped his feet and called his guards to seize Elijah; however, Elijah escaped and immediately fled to Kerith Ravine.

Caw! Caw! I alerted the Crow family of Elijah's arrival. Once they gathered, I announced, "Our guest has arrived. Let's go on a fun-filled scavenger hunt to search for bread and meat to serve our guest. Elijah's stay with us was short. He drank water from the brook and ate bread and meat daily until it was time for him to leave for his next hiding place." The Crow family learned a valuable lesson: *being hospitable can be so much fun!*

Can You Guess The Answer?

1. Name two food items the ravens searched for during their fun-filled scavenger hunt?
2. When a guest visits your home or church, how can you be hospitable to them?

Flying Raven

Supplies

white cardstock
scissors
non-perishable
    canned food
24" diameter of clear
    plastic wrap
rubber band
24" length of ribbon
black crayon
yellow crayon
tape

Preps

Reproduce the Ravens on page 78 on to white cardstock. Cut apart each raven, one per child. Create a sample craft for children to view.

E-Z Steps

1. Hold up sample craft. Instruct children to place the non-perishable canned food in the middle of the clear plastic wrap. Show them how to gather the ends of the plastic wrap together and secure with a rubber band.

2. Ask the children to place the ribbon around the rubber band and knot tie into a bow.

3. Encourage them to color in their Raven's head, body and wings **lightly** using the black crayon (being careful not to cover up the Bible verse) and lastly, color in the Raven's beak using the yellow crayon.

4. Suggest they cut out the Raven and tape to the front of their wrapped food item.

5. Let children read the Bible verse Romans 12:13 aloud, "Share with God's people who are in need. Practice hospitality."

Teachables

If your church does not have a food pantry for the needy, check with neighboring churches where your class can donate their items. Ask the children if they know of a neighbor or friend who may be in need of food due to a loss of a job or illness in the family? Remind the children to practice hospitability like the Raven in our Bible story. Share with God's people who are in need.

SHARE WITH GOD'S
PEOPLE WHO ARE
IN NEED
(ROMANS 12:13)

SHARE WITH GOD'S
PEOPLE WHO ARE
IN NEED
(ROMANS 12:13)

SHARE WITH GOD'S
PEOPLE WHO ARE
IN NEED
(ROMANS 12:13)

Ravens

Hospitality Booklet

Supplies

colored paper
scissors
hole punch
14" thin yarn or ribbon

Preps

Reproduce Hospitality Ideas on page 80 on to colored paper, one per child. Create a sample craft for children to view.

E-Z Steps

1. Let children take turns reading each Hospitality Idea as they cut them out.

2. Hold up sample craft. Show them how to arrange Hospitality Ideas into a booklet form, placing "Practice Hospitality Ideas" page on top. Punch holes where indicated through entire booklet. Insert yarn/ribbon into the holes and then bow tie to secure the pages.

3. Have children look up Romans 12:13 to memorize.

4. Ask children to decide on one Hospitality Idea to work together and complete as a class project. (Go to website addresses if necessary to obtain further information regarding that ministry).

5. Encourage children to work together and complete one Hospitality Idea with their family (*e.g.*, purchase coats, hats and gloves at local garage sales to donate to their local homeless shelter).

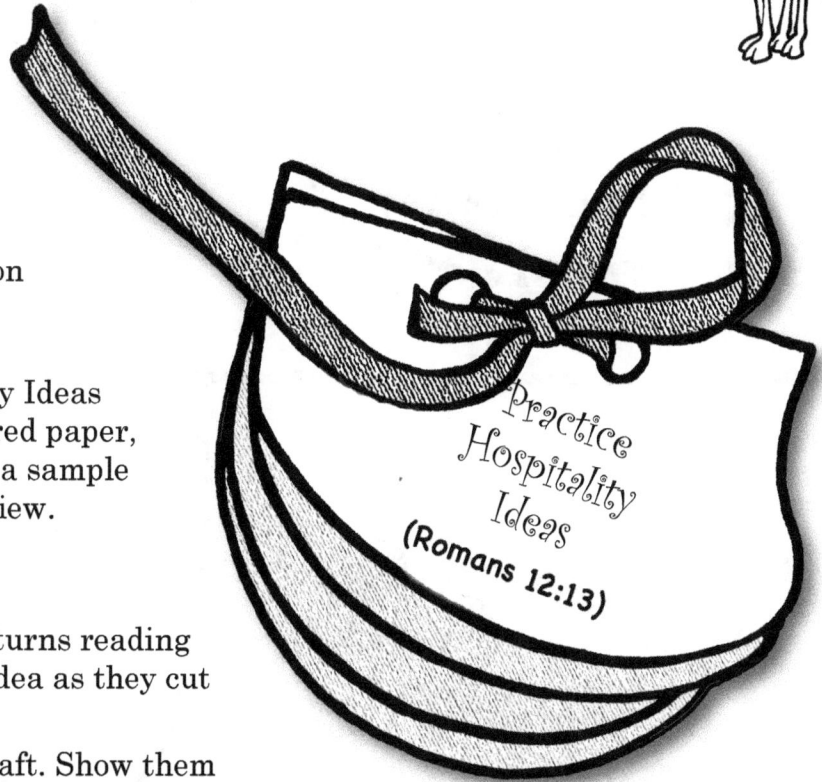

Teachables

Practice being hospitable is the act of being helpful and generous to guests. The ravens in our Bible story created a scavenger hunt to make it fun to share hospitality with their guest Elijah. For example, when your family invites a foreign missionary to stay at your home, find creative fun ways to make them feel at home or hospitable (*e.g.*, serve tacos with a variety of different fillings).

Practice Hospitality Ideas

(Romans 12:13)

Encourage your church to participate in Operation Christmas Child. Sunday school children fill shoe boxes with toys, Bibles and essentials for needy girls/boys in other countries.
www.samaritanspurse.org

Purchase coats, hats and gloves at local garage sales to donate to their local homeless shelter(s).

Search local newspapers for ways to be hospitable (e.g., serve food at food banks, clothes drives, or collect old eyeglasses for the poor).

Encourage neighbors to participate in Orphans Outreach. Collect mittens, hats and scarves for children in orphanages in Russia, Honduras, Guatemala and India.
www.orphansoutreach.org

Ask your church leader to start a non-perishable food pantry or benevolence ministry to share household items, etc. with church or community members.

Hospitality Ideas

Attentive

* * * * * * * * * * *

Memory Verse

Blessed is the man who listens to me, watching daily at my doors, waiting at my doorway (Proverbs 8:34)

Up, Up and Away
Based on 2 Kings 2:1-12
* * * * * * * * * * * * *

Amidst the heavenly clouds, God searched for two helpers for a very special mission. Animals of various sizes, colors and markings humbled in His presence.

I quickly raised my brown, pointy ears and a wave of excitement ran down my back in hopes of being chosen. My hoofs held my wobbly legs steady and my body shook from head to tail like a mini-earthquake. My long flowing mane landed ever so softly on my neck and my tail fluffed-up accordion-style as I was one of two riding animals chosen. Heavenly angels placed a headgear called a bridle over our heads. The bridle fit snug like a glove and connected to a harness to help us pull a two-wheel carriage or chariot. *What a thrill!* We chilled yet stayed attentive to God's sign to leave.

With a touch of God's hand, a whirlwind miraculously formed. *"Neighhhh! Neighhhh!* It's time," I told my riding partner. As the whirlwind began its descent to earth, we followed. On a path of air, we trotted to a fast gallop with the empty chariot behind. *Can you guess what animal we are yet? [pause]*

Down below, the prophet Elijah just finished training soon-to-be prophet Elisha. Elisha was a good student, always wanting to learn, never wanting to leave Elijah's side. Other prophets knew God was coming for Elijah and tried to warn Elisha, "Do you know that the Lord is going to take your master today?" Elisha ignored them and assured Elijah, "I will never leave your side." Elijah answered, "Elisha, I must go alone. Stay here, practice what you have been taught. What can I do for you before I am taken?" Elisha said, "Let me inherit a double portion of your spirit so I may have Godly power to finish your work." Elijah promised, "If you see me taken to heaven, you will inherit my spirit." Suddenly, the whirlwind appeared whipping up the air and separating the two. As God provided skillful horse moves to help us stop the chariot near Elijah's feet, Elisha watched our attentiveness to Elijah. Elijah stepped in, grabbed the reins, and steered toward heaven. *Up, up and away!*

Our attentiveness to Elijah helped Elisha focus more closely on Elijah's ascent to heaven. Elisha was rewarded the double portion of Elijah's spirit. *Oh, what a joy to help!*

Can You Guess The Answer?
1. How did Elisha inherit a double portion of Elijah's spirit?
2. Name one way you can be more attentive to someone else's needs.

Watch for the Lord Plant Stakes

Supplies

colored cardstock
scissors
12 oz. plastic cup
potting soil
resealable plastic bag
plastic tablecloth
glue
colored craft sticks
scallions or green onion
   tops with roots (can
   be purchased at local
   grocery store)

Preps

Reproduce Horses on page 83 on to colored cardstock. Separate each Horse, one per child. Fill the plastic cup one-half full with potting soil. Empty the potting soil into a resealable plastic bag until needed, one per child. Cover the working table with a plastic tablecloth for easy cleanup. Create a sample craft for children to view.

E-Z Steps

1. Instruct children to begin creating their plant stake by gluing two to three different colored craft sticks together (*e.g.*, favorite football team colors).

2. Hold up sample craft. Ask them to cut out the head of the Horse then glue the Horse's head to one end of the joined colored craft sticks.

3. Help them partially fill their plastic cup with potting soil. Place the scallion roots inside and cover the roots with the remaining potting soil.

4. Tell them to insert the plant stake into their soil.

5. Ask children to locate Matthew 24:42 in their Bible to learn the meaning of "Watch for the Lord."

Teachables

The Bible says in Matthew 24:42, "Therefore keep watch, because you do not know on what day your Lord will come." Ready your heart daily. Every time you water your scallion plant and watch it grow, ask forgiveness for your sins, 1 John 1:9.

Matthew 24:42

Watch for the Lord

Matthew 24:42

Watch for the Lord

Matthew 24:42

Watch for the Lord

Matthew 24:42

Watch for the Lord

Matthew 24:42

Watch for the Lord

Matthew 24:42

Watch for the Lord

Horses

Hole-In-One

Supplies

colored paper
12 oz. plastic cup
scissors
30" string
6" x 6" aluminum
    foil square
tape

Preps

Reproduce the Hole-In-One
Verses on page 85 on to
colored paper. **[SAFELY:
Pierce a small hole on the
bottom of the plastic cup,
one per child.]** Cut out the
Hole-In-One Verses, one
verse per child. Create a
sample craft to view.

Each of you
should look not only
to your own interests,
but also to the
interests of others.

PHILIPPIANS 2:4

E-Z Steps

1. Hold up sample craft. Show children how to pull the string through the hole
   at the bottom of their plastic cup. Ask them to knot-tie the string end inside
   the plastic cup several times. Pull the string down at the bottom of the cup
   until the knot inside the cup comes to a stop then tape the string to secure
   in place.

2. Tell them to insert the other string end into the middle of the aluminum
   foil square then crumble up the aluminum foil square into a ball to secure
   string inside.

3. Suggest they tape their Hole-In-One Verse around the body of the cup.

4. Have children read Philippians 2:4 verse on the cup as a reminder for them
   to be attentive to the interests of others.

Teachables

See if you can catch the ball into the opening of the cup. Just as your eyes fix
on the ball going into the cup, the Lord wants us to be attentive to the care and
comfort of others around you.

Each of you should look not only to your own interests, but also to the interests of others.

PHILIPPIANS 2:4

Each of you should look not only to your own interests, but also to the interests of others.

PHILIPPIANS 2:4

Each of you should look not only to your own interests, but also to the interests of others.

PHILIPPIANS 2:4

Each of you should look not only to your own interests, but also to the interests of others.

PHILIPPIANS 2:4

Each of you should look not only to your own interests, but also to the interests of others.

PHILIPPIANS 2:4

Each of you should look not only to your own interests, but also to the interests of others.

PHILIPPIANS 2:4

Each of you should look not only to your own interests, but also to the interests of others.

PHILIPPIANS 2:4

Each of you should look not only to your own interests, but also to the interests of others.

PHILIPPIANS 2:4

Unselfish

* * * * * * * * * *

Memory Verse

*Each of you should look not only to your own interests, but also to the interests of others (**Philippians 2:4**)*

Ferocious Beasts Rewarded

Based on Daniel 6:1-28

* * * * * * * * * * * *

Mmmmmm! The aroma of meat cooking over an open fire sure makes me hungry. "Me too! Who's celebrating?" my den mate curiously asked. King Darius and his newly appointed leaders and helpers. "Is it true the king has a favorite leader?" Yes, his name is Daniel and he will soon rule over the king's *entire* kingdom. The other leaders are jealous and they are looking to bring charges against Daniel, but Daniel is honest and hardworking.

However, the following day, these same jealous leaders came up with a wicked plan. They tricked the king into signing an order, or decree, which said no one in the kingdom should pray to any god or man, except the king, or they would be supper for the ferocious beasts in the den.

Daniel respected the king, but loved God more and continued praying to God three times a day. This encouraged the jealous leaders to run and tell the king of Daniel's actions. Because the king loved Daniel, he tried to ignore their charges, but they pressed him into enforcing his decree. The king reluctantly ordered Daniel to be thrown into the den with the ferocious beasts.

Rooaar! With our taste buds aroused, we stalked, prowled and encircled our prey. "Just in time for supper," we thought. Daniel quickly prayed for help. Suddenly an angel of God appeared. The angel shut our mouths closed and asked us to keep Daniel safe until God's purpose was fulfilled. We unselfishly obeyed and placed God's interests above our own.

The next morning, the king ran to the den in hopes that Daniel was still alive. Daniel was sitting peacefully while petting the longhaired manes of kitten-like animals whose muscular bodies and powerful jaws could snap a man in half. *Can you guess what animal we are yet?* [pause]

The king called to Daniel and he answered: "O king, live forever! My God sent his angel, and he shut the mouths of the lions. They have not hurt me, because I was found innocent in his sight. Nor have I ever done any wrong before you." The king immediately had Daniel released.

The angel of God reopened our mouths and said, *"Job well done!"* The king rewarded our unselfishness and had the jealous leaders and their families thrown in the den for our supper.

The king wrote a new decree: *"This kingdom must fear and reverence the God of Daniel."*

Can You Guess The Answer?

1. What did the lions do to place God's interests above their own?
2. Name one way you can unselfishly place someone else's interest above your own.

Rooaar! What a Cool Gift Bag

Supplies

white cardstock
Ferocious Beasts Rewarded
  Bible story
colored paper
brown lunch bag
tape
chenille stems, two per child
crayons
scissors, glue
cotton ball

Preps

Reproduce the Lion Mane and Face on p. 88 on to white cardstock for each child. Reproduce the *Ferocious Beasts Rewarded* Bible story on p. 86 and Games on p. 89 on to colored paper for each child. Create a sample craft for children to view.

E-Z Steps

1. Hold up sample craft. Show children how to fold and crease the top of their lunch bag inward about two inches (gift bag).

2. Create handles for the gift bag: tape down both ends of one chenille stem to the inside flap on one side of the gift bag. Do the same for the second chenille stem but to the other side of the gift bag.

3. Encourage children to color using these suggestions: Lion Mane: (dark brown or burnt red), Face: (light brown or beige) and Tongue: (pink).

4. Ask children to cut out Lion Mane and Face. Glue the Lion Mane to the outside of the bag. Glue a cotton ball where indicated on the Lion's Mane. Glue the Face to the tip of the cotton ball giving the face a 3-D effect. Allow time for craft to dry. Read Proverbs 3:5 and discuss.

5. Fold the copy of *Ferocious Beasts Rewarded* Bible story and Games page and place them inside the gift bag.

Teachables

Do you know a friend who is not well? Upon your parent's approval, visit with your friend to give them your gift bag. While they are recovering, your friend can read the Bible story and play Games to learn more about God. Once they get well, invite them to Sunday school.

Glue
cotton
*
ball
here

Trust in the Lord (Prov. 3:5)

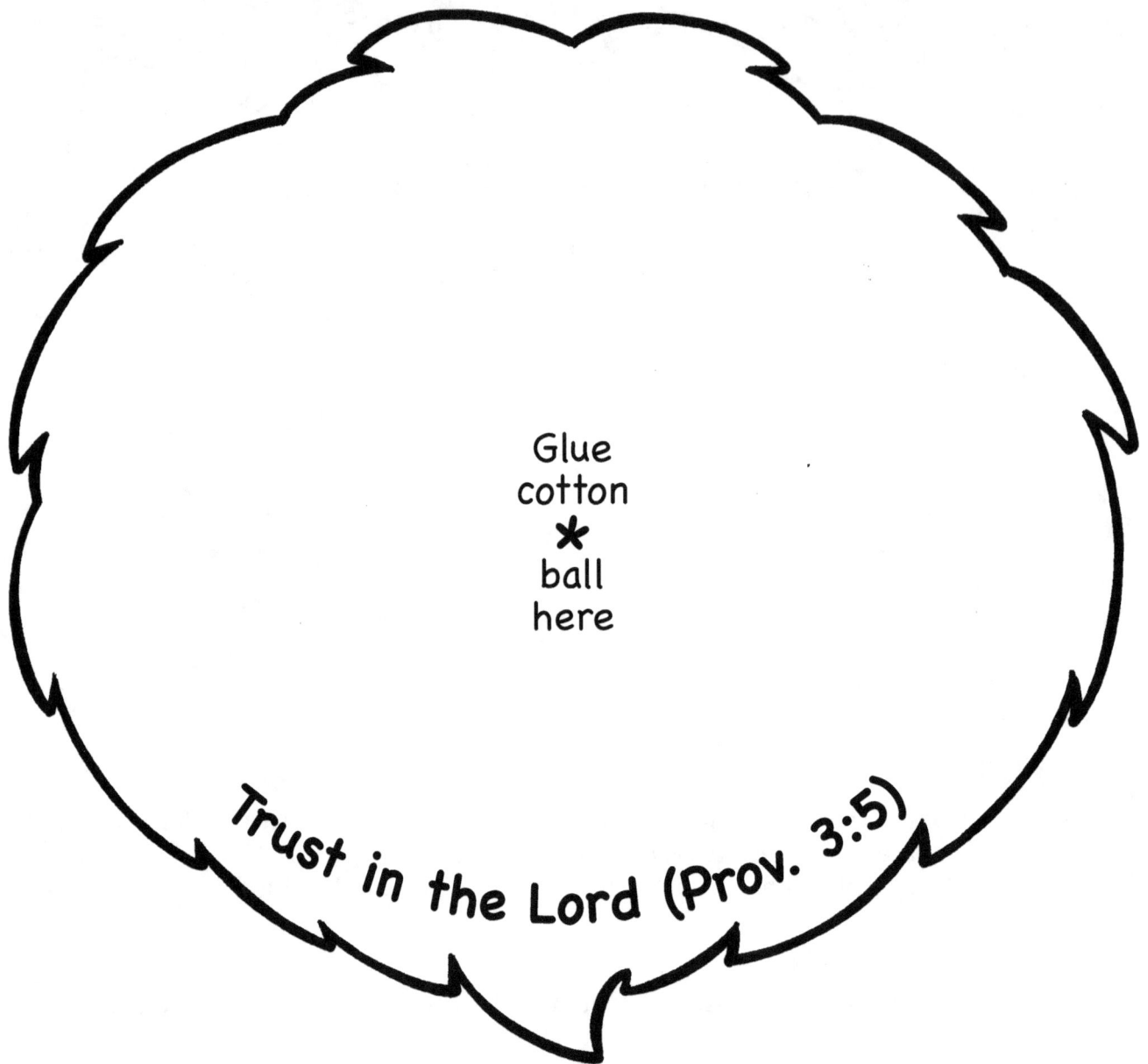

Lion Mane and Face

Get Well! God Loves You!

```
B  G  S  R  E  P  L  E  H
E  N  A  Q  A  N  U  X  U
A  I  D  W  N  E  G  K  N
S  K  I  N  G  D  O  M  G
T  X  F  L  E  A  D  R  R
S  Z  K  I  L  N  E  O  Y
D  F  U  O  Q  I  V  A  A
M  A  N  N  W  E  O  R  R
O  R  D  E  R  L  L  C  P
```

ANGEL
BEASTS
DANIEL
DEN
GOD
HELPERS
HUNGRY
KING
KINGDOM
LION
LOVED
MAN
ORDER
PRAY
ROAR

INSTRUCTIONS:

Highlight or circle the Bible story words listed above in the word search.

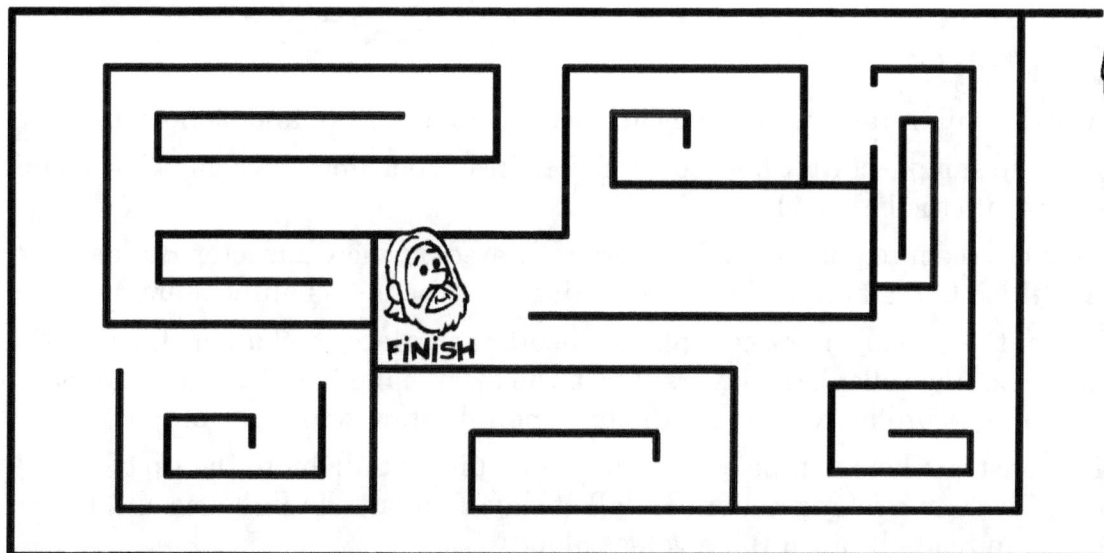

START HERE

FINISH

```
B  G  S  R  E  P  L  E  H
E  N  A  Q  A  N  U  X  U
A  I  D  W  N  E  G  K  N
S  K  I  N  G  D  O  M  G
T  X  F  L  E  A  D  R  R
S  Z  K  I  L  N  E  O  Y
D  F  U  O  Q  I  V  A  A
M  A  N  N  W  E  O  R  R
O  R  D  E  R  L  L  C  P
```

Answer Key To Word Search Above:

89

Games

Fill Up with Godly Character

Supplies

colored cardstock
scissors
colored chenille stems,
    four per child
ball of clay
hole punch
11" diameter colored
    cellophane, two per child
clear tape

Preps

Reproduce Character Builders
on page 91 on to colored cardstock,
one per child. Cut the four chenille
stems in half or eight chenille
stem halves. Create a sample
craft for children to view.

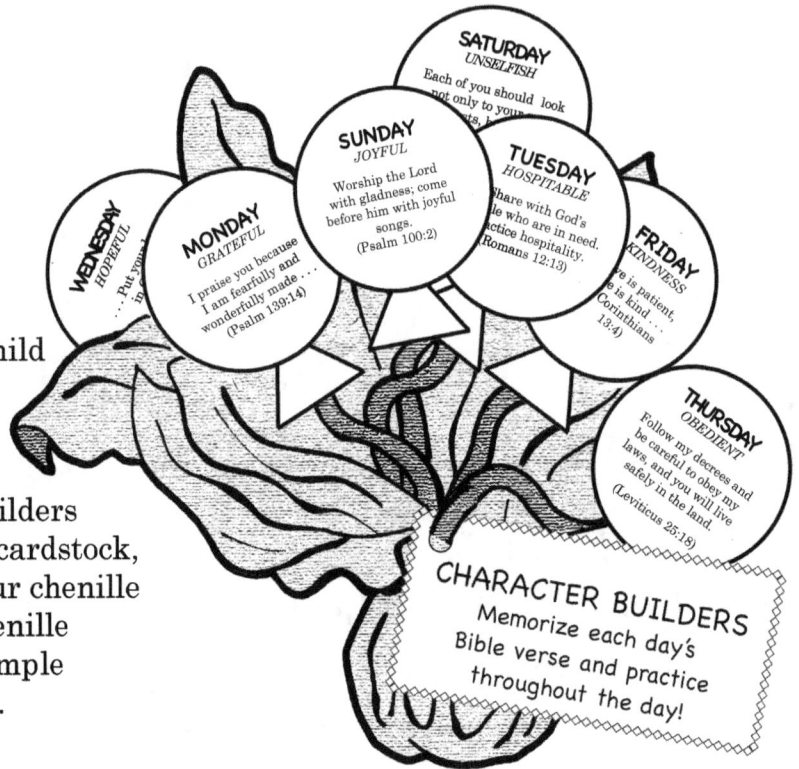

SATURDAY
UNSELFISH
Each of you should look
not only to your
...ts,

SUNDAY
JOYFUL
Worship the Lord
with gladness; come
before him with joyful
songs.
(Psalm 100:2)

TUESDAY
HOSPITABLE
...hare with God's
...le who are in need.
...ctice hospitality.
...Romans 12:13)

WEDNESDAY
HOPEFUL
...Put your...
in...

MONDAY
GRATEFUL
I praise you because
I am fearfully and
wonderfully made . . .
(Psalm 139:14)

FRIDAY
KINDNESS
...e is patient,
...e is kind . . .
...Corinthians
13:4)

THURSDAY
OBEDIENT
Follow my decrees and
be careful to obey my
laws, and you will live
safely in the land
(Leviticus 25:18)

CHARACTER BUILDERS
Memorize each day's
Bible verse and practice
throughout the day!

E-Z Steps

1. Ask the children to cut out the Character Builders Note and Balloons.

2. Hold up sample craft. Show them how to insert one end of seven of the chenille stems into the ball of clay.

3. Instruct them to punch a hole where indicated on the Character Builders Note. Ask them to read the Note before sliding onto the last chenille stem.

4. Direct them to layer the cellophane sheets then place the ball of clay into the middle of the cellophane layers. Wrap the cellophane layers around the ball of clay and secure by twist tying the last chenille stem with the note in place.

5. Demonstrate how to tape each Character Builder Balloon to the tip of each chenille stem sticking out of the ball of clay. Fan out the Balloons and have children read all seven Bible verses aloud.

Teachables

When confronted by the ferocious lions, Daniel prayed and recalled Bible verses from memory. Memorize Bible verses like Daniel for your times of trials. I want to challenge you! Memorize a different Bible verse each day and Fill Up with Godly Character. Practice throughout the day!

Balloons

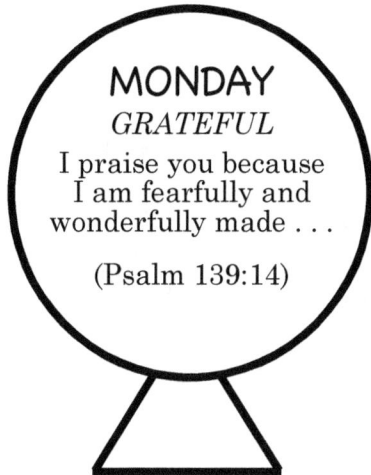

MONDAY
GRATEFUL

I praise you because I am fearfully and wonderfully made . . .

(Psalm 139:14)

TUESDAY
HOSPITABLE

Share with God's people who are in need. Practice hospitality.

(Romans 12:13)

WEDNESDAY
HOPEFUL

. . . Put your hope in God . . .

(Psalm 42:5)

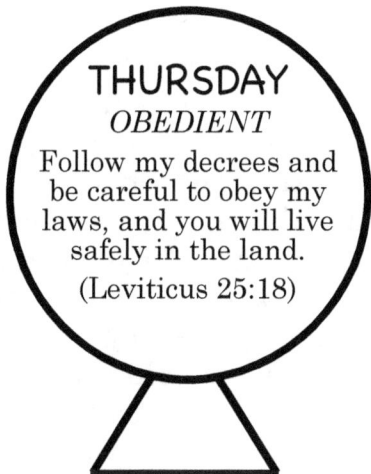

THURSDAY
OBEDIENT

Follow my decrees and be careful to obey my laws, and you will live safely in the land.

(Leviticus 25:18)

FRIDAY
KINDNESS

Love is patient, love is kind . . .

(1 Corinthians 13:4)

SATURDAY
UNSELFISH

Each of you should look not only to your own interests, but also to the interests of others.

(Philippians 2:4)

SUNDAY
JOYFUL

Worship the Lord with gladness; come before him with joyful songs.

(Psalm 100:2)

Note

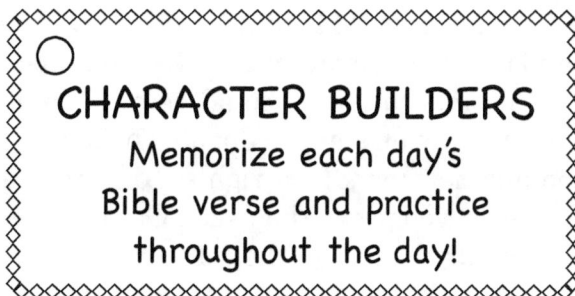

○ **CHARACTER BUILDERS**
Memorize each day's Bible verse and practice throughout the day!

Character Builders

Helpful

* * * * * * * * *

Memory Verse

Brothers, if someone is caught in a sin, you who are spiritual should restore him gently ... **(Galatians 6:1)**

Glad I Can Help, Lord!

Based on Jonah 1, 2 and 3

* * * * * * * * * * * * *

Hee, Hee, Hee! Jonah, that tickles. Oh, please, stop that. You're tickling me. If only you had obeyed God and warned the people of Nineveh to stop their evil ways, you wouldn't be in my belly right now! But you chose to board a ship and run away. Since God had great plans for you, He asked me to bring you back.

Our encounter first began as you boarded a ship for the city of Tarshish. As the ship entered the open waters of the Mediterranean Sea, the ship was caught up in a violent storm. Fear emerged on the faces of the sailors as the crashing waves began breaking up their ship. They cried out for help to their own gods, but the breaking waves crashed only harder and the ship began to sink. Heavy cargo was quickly thrown overboard as the captain woke you and begged for you to call upon your god. Shamefully, you replied, "I am running away from my God, 'the Lord, the God of heaven, who made the sea and the land.' I have sinned against Him and that is why you and your crew are in danger." "Toss me overboard," I heard you plead. The sailors tried one more attempt to row toward shore; however, the ship had a mind of its own as if God was steering the ship. The terrified sailors had no choice but to slip you into the raging waters. Guess what happened? The seas calmed instantly! The sailors knelt and prayed thankfully to your God.

"Yippee! I thought; my mission is upon me," as I quickly swam over to where you were bobbing in the water. I thrust my huge gray body high above the sea, using the powerful might of my enormous tail fin, and landed with a big bad splash. As I surfaced, I blew out air from my blow-hole atop my head, creating a colorful water spray. *Can you guess what animal I am yet? [pause]*

I opened wide for a much-needed breath and *swoosh*; you were sucked up in the swell. You slithered into my belly and tickled as you wiggled to try to escape. I wiggled back, and then made a big splash before disappearing into the sea. I could hear, "Why is it so dark in here? Where am I anyway? *Ewwww!* What is that awful smell?" "Jonah, you're mine," I thought, "plenty of time for you to think how you sinned and how to make it right." For three days and nights, my belly became still. After the third day, I heard you pray. You asked God's forgiveness and promised to obey. God asked me to burp you out onto dry land. I overheard you warn the Nineveh people to stop their evil ways. You shared how God humbled you. They listened and asked for God's forgiveness too. God saw their hearts change and chose not to destroy them. *Glad I Can Help, Lord! What a privilege!*

Can You Guess The Answer?

1. How did God humble Jonah so he would come back to obey Him?
2. How obedient are you when God asks you to help someone else?

92

Glad I Can
Help Magnet

Supplies

white cardstock
scissors, pencil
yellow craft foam
blue craft foam
chenille stem
wiggle eye
fine tip markers
tape, glue
magnet

Glad I Can Help, Lord!

Psalm 121:2

Preps

Reproduce the Whale and Wave on page 94 on to white cardstock. Cut out the Whale, the Whale's Blowhole and the Wave. Place the Whale face down on to the yellow craft foam, trace the Whale and Blowhole, one per child. Place the Wave on to the blue craft foam and trace, one per child. Cut the chenille stem into three 2-inch chenille pieces, three pieces per child. Create a sample craft for children to view.

E-Z Steps

1. Tell the children to cut out the Whale, Whale's Blowhole and Wave from appropriate colored craft foam.

2. Hold up sample craft. Encourage them to glue a wiggle eye or draw an eye on to the face of their Whale. Have them draw eyelashes, eyebrow and a smile on to the Whale's face.

3. Instruct children to curl one end of each 2-inch chenille piece then insert the straight ends into the Whale's Blowhole and tape to the back of the Whale.

4. Ask them to print across the wave, "Glad I Can Help, Lord!" then instruct them to glue the Wave to the bottom of the Whale. Print Psalm 121:2 on the Whale's fin and discuss.

5. Instruct children to glue a magnet to the back of their Whale.

Teachables

Encourage children to place their Whale magnet on their refrigerator at home. Ask them to reflect daily on the words of Psalm 121:2, "My help comes from the Lord, the Maker of heaven and earth." Reflect on how God used the help of a Whale to teach Jonah obedience. How obedient are you when God calls upon your help?

Whale's Blowhole

Whale

Wave

Whale and Wave

O-B-E-Y
Flower Bouquet

Supplies

white cardstock
ball of clay
plastic baby food
    container w/o lid
glue stick, scissors
tissue paper scraps
light colored crayons,
    four per child
colored craft sticks,
    four per child
black permanent marker
green Easter grass

God Parent Teacher Police

O B E Y

John 15:12

Preps

Reproduce Tulips on page 96 on to white cardstock. Separate the Tulips on the dashed line, four per child. Create a sample craft for children to view.

E-Z Steps

1. Ask children to place the ball of clay inside the plastic baby food container.

2. Tell them to glue tissue paper scraps around the body of the plastic baby food container. Allow time for craft to dry.

3. Encourage children to color each Tulip a different color. Cut out and glue each Tulip to the tip of a different colored craft stick.

4. Hold up sample craft. Tell them to print one letter from the word O B E Y on to a different craft stick (*e.g.,* God (O), Parents (B), Teachers (E) and Police (Y)) (see illustration above). Insert craft sticks into the clay ball so the letters spell the word, OBEY.

5. Glue green Easter grass over the clay ball. Print John 15:12 on the body of the baby food container. Look up John 15:12 and discuss how to love each other as God loves us.

Teachables

Do you find it difficult to O-B-E-Y God, Parents, Teachers or Police? God says, love each other as he loves us. This is God's command. To love others, especially those in authority, we must be obedient to them as well as helpful when they need our help. Place your flower bouquet where you can view it daily, as a reminder to O-B-E-Y.

God

Parents

Teachers

Police

God

Parents

Teachers

Police

Tulips

www.ingramcontent.com/pod-product-compliance
Lightning Source LLC
LaVergne TN
LVHW081319060426
835509LV00015B/1592